MASTERPIECES

LIBRARY
ARCHITECTURE + DESIGN

MASTERPIECES

MANUELA ROTH

LIBRARY
ARCHITECTURE + DESIGN

BRAUN

PREFACE.

At the beginning of the new millennium library architecture must measure up to new challenges. The increasing digitalization of our daily lives and the supply of information via the internet must be taken into account for the use of library visitors. New forms with increased requirements profiles must be found to augment the old fashioned book shelves. Libraries were formerly considered simply as storehouses of knowledge. They were places of keeping and collecting books in a building with a prestigious appearance. During the last century the ever growing extent of the collections necessitated larger, connected stacks areas in order to most efficiently store the books.

Simultaneously at the beginning of the new millennium information everyone had access to information from everywhere. One can find out about the latest developments the fastest online, and books are being digitalized and presented in the internet. But there is still a great demand for books and the building of libraries continues, commissioned by public as well as institutional sponsors. The demands are as varied as the results depicted in this book.

The library has become transformed from a quiet, introverted building into an information provider for the promotion of communication. It has become an important social interface where users contact each other, exchange information and work together.

Contemporary architecture must respond to the fact that almost all visitors process the information they receive on their laptops. Inviting, open and varied work places are being provided like the "readers' terraces" in the Jacob and Wilhelm Grimm Center in Berlin. Max Dudler won the architecture competition and in 2009 the building was opened. The building looks monolithic, a rectangular structure with natural stone cladding. Different wide window openings lend a rhythm to the façade. In conjunction with the interior the architecture achieves design unity. Shelves, work places and seating areas are oriented to the building grid. However the heart of the center is the impressive large reading room. It is built up in tiers like a terrace, from the ground floor to the fourth floor and is supplied with natural light by skylights. An atmosphere of relaxation but also concentration is the result. A total of approximately 1,250 work places are available, either as single or group work places. But even this number can not absorb the onslaught of users who have been overwhelming the facility every day since it was opened.

The "Rolex Learning Center" in Lausanne of the Japanese architects Sanaa uses another concept. The architects understand the library, which is part of the Technical University, figuratively as a kind of "landscape of education". The user becomes the traveller, moving through an architectural landscape with slight elevations and hills and valleys. A "free space" has been created which allows for the necessary latitude for learning. One can wander about through spaces which are not separated by partitions. There are no prescribed paths. Along the way one can encounter book shelves, work places, a café and plenty of seating possibilities. Thoughts are permitted to ramble. There are small glass cubicles to which one can withdraw for concentrated group work. The architecture is on the move and seeks to motivate the visitor to learn communication and cooperation.

Masterpieces Library Architecture + Design presents a collection of contemporary buildings from around the world with many answers to this fascinating building task.

PROJECTS.

www.2ap.it

Client: IED - European Design Institute, **Completion:** 2009, **Gross floor area:** 230 m², **Photos:** Sebastiano Costanzo/Rome.

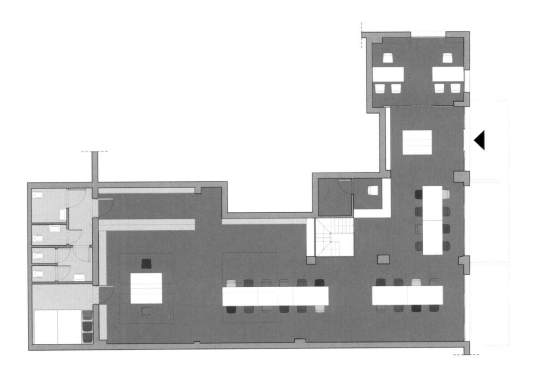

Left: Study area. | Right: Plan of the Ground floor.

The project was to renovate the existing library. The goal of the architects was to create a space dedicated to study, the access to books and magazines and at the same time, the editors' office of the magazine published by the European Institute of Design. Also needed was a multifunctional and flexible space capable of hosting seminars and conferences. The renovated spaces are characterized by a minimalistic design, defined by a colored floor and by painting it black, creating a sort of false ceiling . Part of the walls, including all the ventilation installation, and the hanging circular lamps were designed specifically for the renovation.

From left to right, from above to below:
Entrance area, Reception desk, Working desk.
Right: Library space.

LIBRARY AM GUISANPLATZ,
BERNE, SWITZERLAND

ALB ARCHITEKTENGEMEINSCHAFT AG WITH DAVID BOSSHARD

www.alb-arch.ch

Client: Bundesamt für Bauten und Logistik, Bern, **Completion:** 2005, **Gross floor area:** 4,060 m², **Photos:** Marco Schibig, Bern.

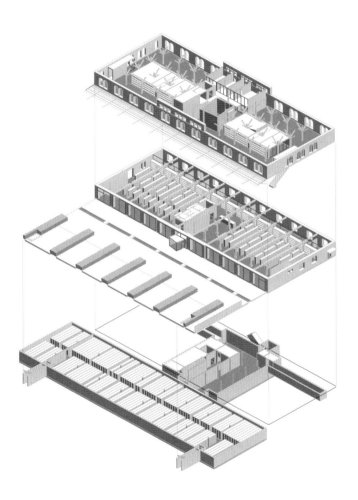

Left: Library wall. | Right: Axonomety of the library with with underground storeroom.

The original armory from 1893/1910 consists of two hall-like floors with an expressive wood construction and is classified as worthy of preservation. The architects have thematically incorporated the spatial appearance of the hall with the brick shell, the woodwork, the hard flooring and the large gateways on the ground floor, where they located an open access library and reading places. On the upper floor the various usage requirements are accommodated by freely situated wooden boxes. The renovation fulfils the Minergie standard. The former forecourt has been evolved into a large scale urban garden, leaving a presentiment of the space for book storage beneath it.

SWISS NATIONAL LIBRARY,
BERNE, SWITZERLAND

ALB ARCHITEKTENGEMEINSCHAFT AG WITH DAVID BOSSHARD AND OLIVIER MOSSET

www.alb-arch.ch

Client: Bundesamt für Bauten und Logistik, Bern, **Completion:** 2001, **Gross floor area:** 18,485 m², **Photos:** Marco Schibig, Bern, Schweizer Luftwaffe (23).

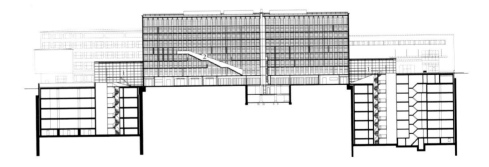

Left: Main entrance of the library. | Right: Longitudinal section.

The Swiss National Library, completed in 1931, is an important testimony of modern architecture in Switzerland. Along with the careful restoration of the original substance, the reorganization of the library necessitated additional usages. These new functions were installed with minimal, elegant components in the original clear, sober spaces on the ground floor.

The new open access library and a reading room for the Swiss National Literature Archive were located in the former warehouse, an industrial looking concrete structure. A layering arising from the close positioning of the columns in the lower floors allows for a multi-story play of space and light. The cascade staircase, which guides the visitors to the upper floors, belongs to this spatial structure.

Left: Double height facade in the library. Right: The true to original renovated reading room.

From left to right, from above to below:
Connection building, North facade of the original store house,
Garden across the underground store house east.
Right: Aerial view of the situation.

CHILEAN NATIONAL LIBRARY FOUNDERS HALL,
SANTIAGO, CHILE

www.diav.cl

Client: National Library, **Completion:** 2009, **Gross floor area:** 400 m², **Photos:** Eduardo Cifuentes.

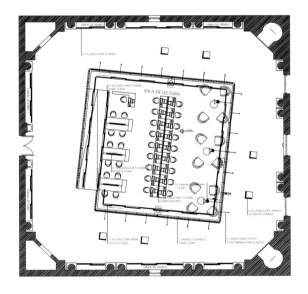

Left: Elevated and lit volume. | Right: Illumination plan.

After winning the open competition, the reading room and exhibition spaces were realized in the Founders Lounge of the National Library – the main space in this national heritage building. The design also involves a new lighting concept. The architects proposed a glazed volume elevated over the ground level, which contrasts and highlights the classical architecture context. This volume is structured by a silk-screened glass with texts containing the names of the main Chilean writers. It is illuminated with cold white light, providing the contrast of contemporary intervention with the classical architecture of the room, whose warm white lighting highlights the most important architectural elements such as arches, pillars and the dome.

From left to right, from above to below:
Bird's eye view, Detail of glass wall, Lighting at night.
Right: Reading area.

GROSUPLJE PUBLIC LIBRARY,
GROSUPLJE, SLOVENIA

ARCHITECTURE: MATEJ BLENKUŠ,
MILOŠ FLORIJANČIČ (ABIRO)
INTERIOR DESIGN: NENA GABROVEC,
ARNE VEHOVAR, KAJA LIPNIK VEHOVAR

www.abiro.net

Client: Grosuplje Municipality, **Completion:** 2007, **Gross floor area:** 1,750 m², **Photos:** Miran Kambič /
Radovljica, Slovenia.

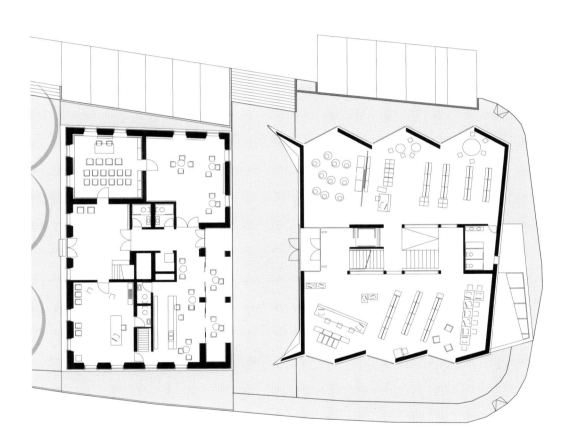

Left: View from North-east. | Right: Ground floor plan of both buildings.

The existing library operated in an old town house, the
only preserved representative of quality architecture
from 19th century in Grosuplje and protected as a
listed building. Next to it the new wing was added,
twice as large. Inside it a modern, open and fluid
library space, designed with efficient use of light and
energy in mind. The façade of the annex stretches like
an accordion across the plot and with the repetitive
exchange of glass and wall surfaces opens the new
library space towards the ambiance of the town's
center. Neutrality and monumentality are repeated in
a manner that allows the pavilion to become "grown"
into the town's fibre and its unimposing presence allows the old building to retain the dominant role.

Left: Passage between the old and the new building, View of the new buildings at night, Passage between both buildings. Right: Detail of façade.

From left to right, from above to below:
Reading/working area, Vertical communications are a part of
open library space, Connecting corridor between both buildings.
Right: Reading area.

THOMPSON LIBRARY RENOVATION,
COLUMBUS (OH), USA

ACOCK ASSOCIATES ARCHITECTS – ARCHITECT OF RECORD

www.acock.com
Client: The Ohio State University, **Completion:** 2009, **Gross floor area:** 28,000 m², **Photos:** Brad Feinknopf 2009 / Columbus (OH).

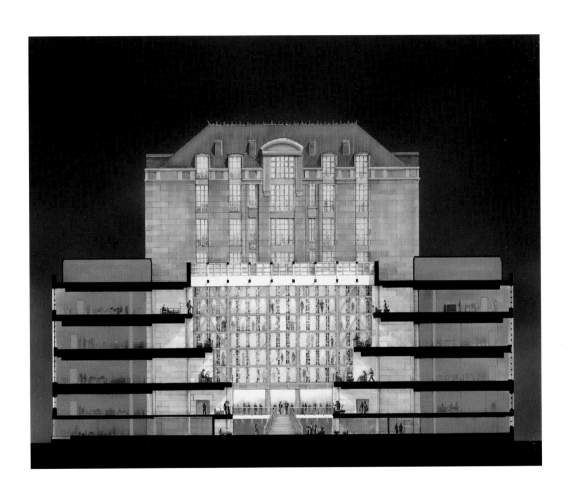

Left: Elevation west Addition. | Right: Section of the atrium.

The design challenge was to modernize and enlarge the main library of the Ohio State University into a technologically relevant, contemporary study and research center. In blending and merging the original construction of 1913 with the additions of 1950 and 2009, the design explores a timeline of building styles that supports endearing images of a traditional library as it evolves into a technological and collaborative information center. The library's print collection is prominently displayed. Interior spaces and circulation are organized around the stack tower. Atria with large skylights introduce grand daylighted volumes deep in the center of a large building footprint. A variety of study/research/collaborative spaces surround the collection.

Left: South-west corner of new addition. Right: New West "Buckeye Reading Room".

From left to right, from above to below:
West Atrium and Grand Stair, West Atrium and Flying Stair,
Outside of the "Buckeye Reading Room", Histroic Reading Room
after renovation.
Right: Exhibition area.

THE UNIVERSITY OF HELSINKI
CITY CAMPUS LIBRARY,
HELSINKI, FINLAND

ANTTINEN OIVA ARCHITECTS LTD

www.aoa.fi

Client: University of Helsinki, **Completion:** 2012, **Gross floor area:** 31,700 m², **Photos:** AOA.

Left: Exterior view from railway station. | Right: Sketch, view from below reading balconies.

The University of Helsinki is developing its library structure by joining together five faculty libraries, which are presently dispersed in different parts of the city center, to form a single administrative unit. The largest academic library in Finland will be created in the historically important Hirvi (Elk) city block. The new library building complements the urban block by adding a curved brick façade, integrated within the street line formed by the adjacent buildings. The dense fenestration grid blurs the standard floor division. Together with the large arched openings, it gives the library a distinct appearance from the outside. The terraced reading galleries in the interior are also visible in the façade.

From left to right, from above to below:
Central void, Exterior view from Vuorikatu street, 5th floor reading
balcony, View from 5th floor reading balcony.
Right: Main lobby.

CURNO PUBLIC LIBRARY AND AUDITORIUM,
CURNO, ITALY

ARCHEA ASSOCIATI

www.archea.it

Client: Comune di Curno, **Completion:** 2009, **Gross floor area:** 1,960 m², **Photos:** Pietro Savorelli.

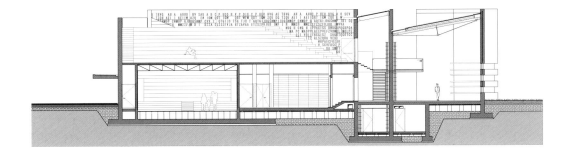

Left: Exterior view. | Right: Section.

The project is a monolith of concrete stained with iron oxides, completely decorated with bas-relief engraved letters. The structure, divided by a long corridor bounded by a concrete double wall, contains the two main functions: the Auditorium and the Library. The central corridor constitutes the true backbone of the project. In the basement floor there is a long and spacious warehouse for books with shelves made of commercial metal sections. From the corridor-periodicals room – on two levels, fully illuminated from above by a long skylight the visitors access the main reading room: a doubleheight space illuminated by a few banded windows that extend the entire length of the reading room façade surface, and by two skylights.

From left to right, from above to below:
Central corridor, Entrance area,
Exterior side view, Main reading room.
Right: Detail of the façade, engraved letters.

LIBRARY IN NEMBRO,
NEMBRO, ITALY

ARCHEA ASSOCIATI

www.archea.it

Client: Comune di Nembro, **Completion:** 2007, **Gross floor area:** 1,875 m², **Photos:** Pietro Savorelli.

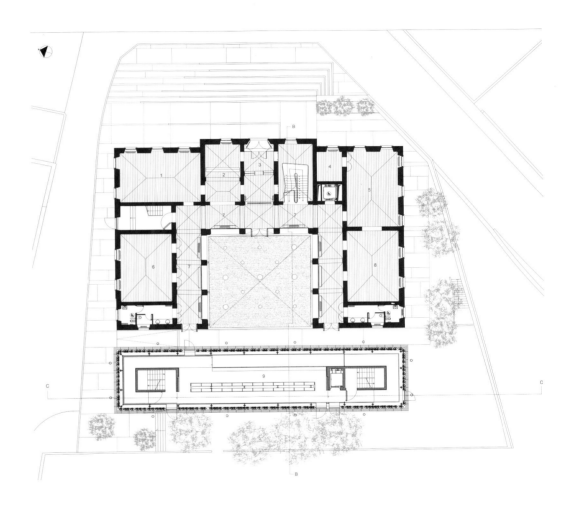

Left: Exterior view of new wing and original building. | Right: Floor plan.

The city requested that the original building, erected in 1897, be renovated and turned into a library. The architectural character of the structure, closed on three sides, and the need for more space made it necessary to add a new wing. The new wing, detached from the old structure on all sides, is connected with the existing building through the base-ment. Its completely transparent body is characterized by a façade in 40 x 40 centimeters earthenware tiles, glazed in carmine red. This construction makes it possible to screen and filter the daylight. While the use of earthenware evokes traditional building methods, the building at the same time looks extremely contemporary.

From left to right, from above to below:
Façade with ceramic tiles, Interior view from the upper floor of the
new wing, Library on the upper floor, Ceramic tiles.
Right: No visible connection between old and new construction.

ÍLHAVO CITY LIBRARY,
ÍLHAVO, PORTUGAL

ARX PORTUGAL ARQUITECTOS

www.arx.pt

Client: Ílhavo Municipality, **Completion:** 2005, **Gross floor area:** 3,200 m², **Photos:** FG+SG – Fernando Guerra Photographer.

Left: Exterior view. | Right: Cross section lobby.

Ílhavo City Library is located in the remains of a noble house from the 17th-18th century. From the original building only the main façade and the chapel, both in ruins, were left. The preliminary program contains three autonomous nuclei: Library, Chapel and Youth Forum. The limits of the manor and the line of the old façade were chosen as an anchorage point, where administrative areas and programmes were placed, restoring the character of the original building. There is nevertheless a clear identification of the new, which exists in symbiosis with the pre-existence. The design of the reading rooms establish direct morphological relations with the surroundings, in context thus making the architecture work as a closing.

From left to right, from above to below:
Main entrance, Interior view of the entrance area,
Exterior of the new construction.
Right: Reading room.

DAVID WILSON LIBRARY,
LEICESTER, UNITED KINGDOM

ASSOCIATED ARCHITECTS LLP

www.associated-architects.co.uk
Client: University of Leicester, **Completion:** 2008, **Gross floor area:** 15,000 m², **Photos:** Martine Hamilton Knight / Nottingham.

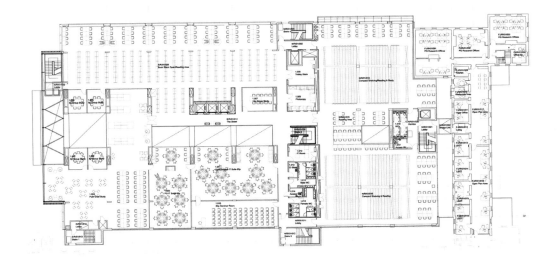

Left: Main entrance and podium. | Right: Floor plan of first floor.

The requirements of the university were very clear in its brief. The Library should be an excellent environment for people as well as for books, putting the needs of students and researchers at the very heart of the project. The relaxation of the strict environmental criteria of the storage of books in lieu of natural ventilation is an example. There is a tendency for people to assume that libraries are just storehouses rather than workplaces. This emphasis on the users of the building suggested the key aspects of the design should give it a surprise factor, a lot of natural light, a layout which was easy to navigate, having local control of services, being energy efficient, and have a high quality of materials and finish. All of these aims have been successfully achieved.

From left to right, from above to below:
Feature lighting in new atrium, Rear atrium formed at connection
with listed building, Mono crystalline PV array within glazed brise
soleil on south façade.
Right: Post graduate reading room.

L'ALBATROS – MÉDIATHÈQUE D'ARMENTIÈRES,
ARMENTIÈRES, FRANCE

BÉAL & BLANCKAERT
ARCHITECTES ASSOCIÉS

www.beal-blanckaert.com

Client: Mairie d'Armentières, **Completion:** 2005, **Gross floor area:** 2900 m², **Photos:** Pierre Emmanuel Rouxel (60, 62 b. l.), Jean Pierre Duplan (62 a., 63), Julien Lanoo (62 b. l.).

Left: View from the street. | Right: Section.

The new Media Center provides the city of Armentières with a performant tool with regard to reading and new cultural media. Culture, urbanity and architecture are the major actors of a city in the architects' eyes. Through the use of unifying materials, like shining stainless steel in the roof and in the façades, and wood in the interior of the building, supporting a strong formal presence, the architectural writing of Béal and Blanckaert is stated in terms of "narration" and expressionism convenient to a formal interpretation. This rule ensures the building an appropriate dimension, in a horizontal vaulted envelope that folds and unfolds itself in order to meet the client's requirements and to absorb the differences of heights of the programs.

From left to right, from above to below:
Interior view, Exterior view, View from the backyard,
Interior view from the second floor.
Right: Façade of stainless steel.

UNIVERSITY MENSA AND LIBRARY LEIPZIG,
LEIPZIG, GERMANY

BEHET BONDZIO LIN ARCHITEKTEN

www.2bxl.com

Client: Staatsbetrieb Sächsisches Immobilien- und Baumanagement Leipzig SIB NL Leipzig II, **Completion:** 2009, **Gross floor area:** ca. 70.000 m², **Photos:** Christian Richters / artur.

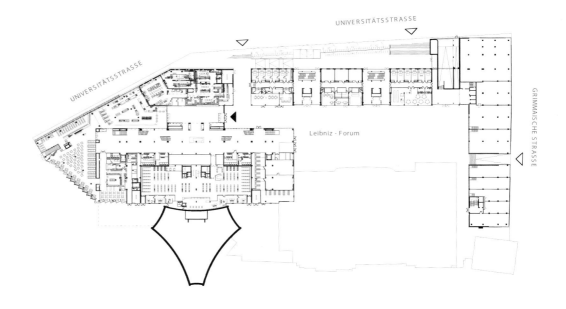

Left: New Mensa building. | Right: Ground floor plan.

The building is one of the old buildings of the 1970's era campus. Its interior was marked by brick-clad foyer walls as well as the Scandinavian charm in the library. The library was connected to the foyer by a central atrium and the basement expanded in order to accommodate approximately 100,000 volumes, an extensive magazine collection, e-books, and 500 work places. It maintains a quiet and concentrated atmosphere with the bright wall surfaces and wood trim. The starting point for the architects for the conception of the inner city university complex was the reintegration in the city structure on the basis of the historical blocks with their alleys, passageways and courtyards. The connection of the buildings of the campus is accomplished by the dominant bright façades surrounding a dark plinth.

From left to right, from above to below:
Atrium of the library, warm materials were used for the interior,
Exterior view of the new building.
Right: Exterior view of the library and auditorium.

KAZAKHSTAN NATIONAL LIBRARY,
ASTANA, KAZAKHSTAN

BIG ARCHITECTS

www.big.dk
Client: Kazakhstan Presidential Office, Completion: 2012, Gross floor area: 33,000 m², Photos: BIG – Bjarke Ingels Group.

Left: Exterior view. | Right: Diagram of the structure.

To design the Foundation and Library of the First President of the Republic of Kazakhstan is more than a common architectural challenge. The National Library will be one of the cornerstones of Kazakh nation building, and a leading institution representing the Kazakh national identity. The new National Library in Astana shall not only store history but also project new futures for the nation and its new capital. In the library researchers will be able to study the history of the Kazakh culture and language present in the massive collection of books, magazines and film. The park around the library is designed like a living library of trees, plants, minerals and rocks allowing visitors to experience a cross section of Kazakhstan's natural landscape.

From left to right, from above to below:
View from inside, Interior views.
Right: Exterior view.

LIBRARY IN DENDERMONDE,
DENDERMONDE, BELGIUM

BOB361 ARCHITECTS

www.bob361.com

Client: City of Dendermonde – Dexia Bank, **Completion:** 2010, **Gross floor area:** 6,300 m², **Photos:** André Nullens.

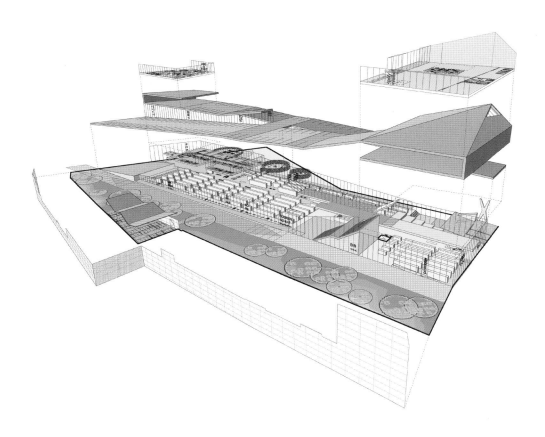

Left: Exterior view from the roof. | Right: Organigramm.

The building site is situated between the main road of the city of Dendermonde and the green bank of the river Dender. Two "ground level-connected" landscapes are superimposed and manipulated. Together they limit the interior library space. The rooftop - square acts as a transit space for the flow of cars and people. It folds to get natural light into the underlying spaces. Between roof and floor the library forms a big "rippling" space in which the furniture does not block the general overview. Therefore the floor is lowered where the book collections are installed. The central circulation-strip services the different collections and is naturally lit.

From left to right, from above to below:
Reception area, Interior view from the upper floor, Exterior view.
Right: Interior view.

LIBRARY KÖPENICK,
BERLIN, GERMANY

BRUNO FIORETTI MARQUEZ
ARCHITEKTEN

www.bfm-architekten.de
Client: Land Berlin, **Completion:** 2008, **Gross floor area:** 2,362 m², **Photos:** ORCH, Alessandra Chemollo.

Left: Exterior view. | Right: Elevation.

The library rooms are located on the ground floor, accessible via a generous foyer. One enters the reading area through a two story high room, with a view of the Spree through a large window. The book cases are located along the walls and in the one story areas, while the reading booths have been placed in the two story areas. The building consists of four elements, each of which is keyed by a building material: Exterior walls (masonry), roof (wood construction), interior room (concrete structure), furniture (MDF and books). The dynamic profile of the roof, one of the most important hallmarks of the building, is executed as staggered folds in white laminated timber. Natural light from the skylights penetrates deep into the reading room through narrow transverse ribs.

From left to right, from above to below:
Detail of the brick façade, Interior views.
Right: Interior view with ceiling.

CITY LIBRARY OF POPERINGE "DE LETTERBEEK",
POPERINGE, BELGIUM

www.buro2.be
Client: City of Poperinge, **Completion:** 2006, **Gross floor area:** 1,639 m², **Photos:** Koen Van Damme (80, 82 a.), Axioma Lighting (82 b., 83).

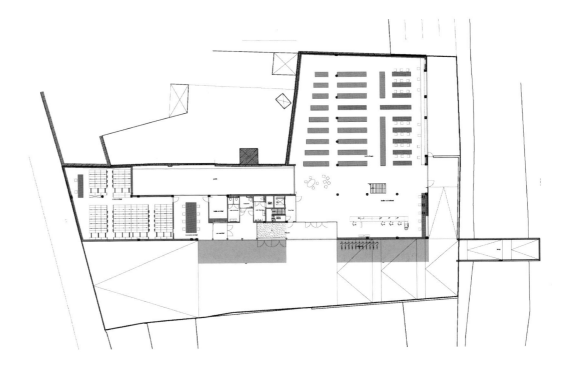

Left: Exterior view. | Right: Ground floor plan.

BURO II designed a solid box with three façades. The building itself is open and transparent. One of the most significant consequences of combining the architectural and the interior design from the beginning, is the presence of the high windows on the north side of the building. The library benefits from the constant northern light that will not damage the books. Every space in the library provides a view of the municipal park. On the ground floor, the shelves were positioned to draw the gaze of the visitor automatically to the outside view. In the first floor, the shelves have been placed to provide a view over the lower floor. In the open and airy space on the ground floor, shelves have been set up as logically as possible, making the need for signage as minimal as possible.

From left to right, from above to below:
Exterior view, Exterior view of the entrance.
Right: Interior view.

INFORMATION, COMMUNICATION AND MEDIA CENTER OF THE TFH WILDAU,
WILDAU, GERMANY

CHESTNUTT_NIESS ARCHITEKTEN

www.chestnutt-niess.de

Client: Schwartzkopf Werke für Herstellung von Lokomotiven, **Completion:** 2007, **Gross floor area:** 4,265 m²,
Photos: Werner Huthmacher / artur.

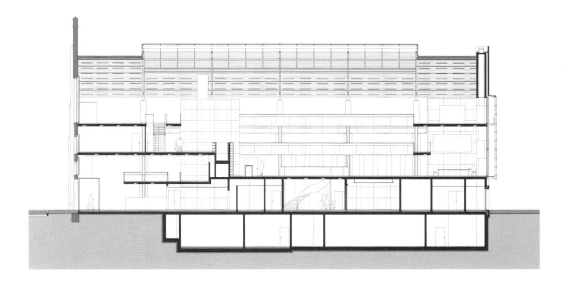

Left: Exterior view. | Right: Section.

The building geometry of the historic hall is continued by a contemporary extension which expresses the new use and which underscores its urban developmental position between the college and the historically listed industrial facility as gateway to the former workers' settlement. For the first time the culminating alignment of the long gable front of the overall facility emerges as an urban developmental boundary. The conversion and extension of the existing hall into a media center is made possible while respecting the historically intended total volume. The architectural language of this "continuation" refers to and extends the original structure, but makes use of the materiality and forms of current building practice.

From left to right, from above to below:
Exterior view, Interior view upper floor, Workstaions.
Right: Interior view of the library.

CULTURE HOUSE AND LIBRARY,
COPENHAGEN, DENMARK

COBE

www.cobe.dk

Client: Copenhagen Municipality, **Completion:** 2010, **Gross floor area:** 2,000 m², **Photos:** COBE.

Left: Exterior view. | Right: Ground floor plan.

The Northwest area of Copenhagen is located in the diverse and lively transition zone between a dense urban area and villa neighbourhoods. Even though many people live and work in this multi-ethnic part of Copenhagen, it is mainly a transit area for many residents. The new Culture House + Library is composed of several elements: Rethinking and modernisation of an existing culture house, a merger of two newer libraries, and the addition of a new culture hall, together forming an enormous potential as a new Culture House for the whole area. This can contribute a significant and attractive cultural institution lacking in the neighbourhood, today, creating a strong sense of community.

From left to right, from above to below:
Exterior view at night.
Right: Interior view.

FH CAMPUS LIBRARY VIENNA,
VIENNA, AUSTRIA

DELUGAN MEISSL
ASSOCIATED ARCHITECTS

www.deluganmeissl.at

Client: FH Campus Wien, Planungs-, Finanzierungs- und Errichtungs GmbH, **Completion:** 2009, **Gross floor area:** 24,000 m², **Photos:** Hertha Hurnaus.

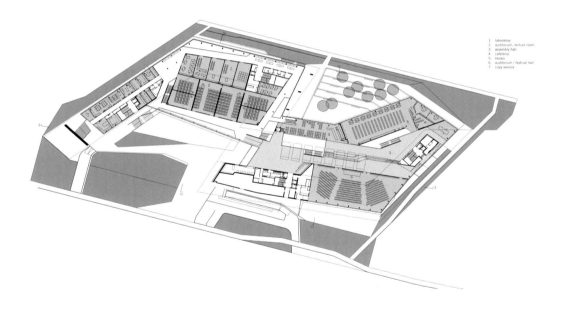

1 laboratory
2 auditorium, lecture room
3 assembly hall
4 cafeteria
5 library
6 auditorium / festival hall
7 copy service

Left: Exterior view of the entrance. | Right: Ground floor plan.

The building was erected in just eighteen months, opening in the summer of 2009. Rhythmically occurring height differences in the façade of the stand-alone, horizontally structured building determine the horizontal window configuration. The primary uses, like the information central, auditorium, library, ballroom and cafeteria, are arranged in a consistent sequence along the varying levels of height in the interior. Bridges, seating steps, designated functional areas and open spaces alternate, providing a structure of clear orientation. The monochrome appearance of the interior is relieved in a play of light and shadow by a constant back and forth of black and white as well as varied degrees of surface sheen.

From left to right, from above to below:
Cafeteria and atrium, Interior view of the library.

MULTIMEDIA LIBRARY AND THEATER,
ALFORTVILLE, FRANCE

DESO ARCHITECTS

www.deso-architecture.com

Client: Communauté d'agglomération de la Plaine Centrale du Val-de-Marne, **Completion:** 2007, **Gross floor area:** 4,544 m², **Photos:** Hervé Abbadie.

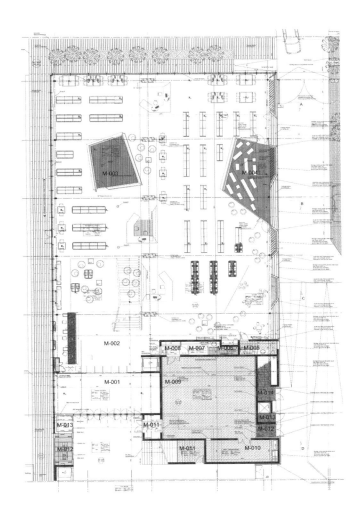

Left: Exterior view at night. | Right: Ground floor plan.

The Alfortville City Cultural Center combines a multimedia library, a theater with 450 seats and a multi purpose activity room. The multimedia library is organized around 2 levels which provide majestic height and verticality. All of the reading rooms have glass roofs to illuminate the spaces with natural light. The glass façade is complemented by a Japanese "engawa" footpath. The building seems alive, and the transparency of the façade invites the people passing by to come in. At night, the glow from the inside makes the building a landmark in the city. The project boasts a coherent assembly of renewable energies, especially with the installation of a heat pump to optimise energy consumption.

Actualité-Presse

Art-Musique-Cinéma

Adultes

Jeunes

From left to right, from above to below:
Exterior perspective at night, View inside at night, Interior view of
the library, Interior view first floor.
Right: Interior view of the entrance area.

DIOCESAN LIBRARY,
MÜNSTER, GERMANY

MAX DUDLER

www.maxdudler.de
Client: Bischöfliches Generalvikariat Münster, **Completion:** 2005, **Gross floor area:** 14,300 m², **Photos:** Stefan Müller, Berlin.

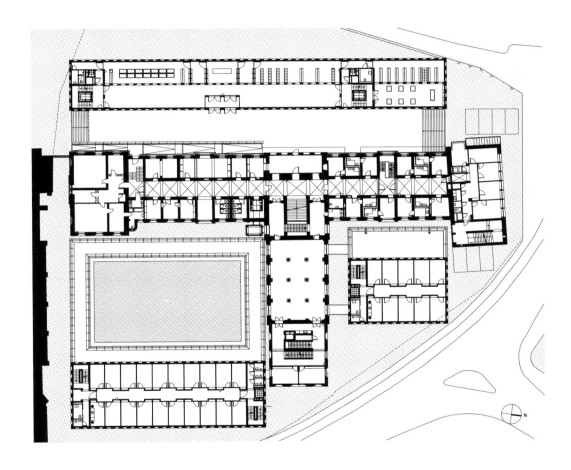

Left: Interior courtyard Überwasserkirche. | Right: Ground floor plan.

The Münster diocesan library is the largest specialized library in Germany. The new ensemble consists of three cubes, one of which incorporates the library. Its 70 meter long rectangular shape is a striking feature of the urban landscape, particularly since the length corresponds with the administrative building across the way. Inner spaces are created by the disposition of the building cubes: the alley between the library and the seminary, a courtyard and a cloister-like priests' garden. All the new buildings are clad with local light colored natural stone and overlaid with a completely uniform grid of deep recessed, high aperture windows. The façade structure resembles a giant book case.

From left to right, from above to below:
Alley, Detail of façade, Shelves, Santini reading room.
Right: Main reading room.

JACOB AND WILHELM GRIMM CENTER,
BERLIN, GERMANY

MAX DUDLER

www.maxdudler.de

Client: Humboldt-Universität zu Berlin, **Completion:** 2009, **Gross floor area:** 37,460 m², **Photos:** Stefan Müller, Berlin.

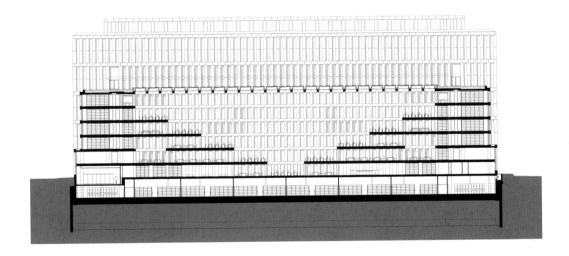

Left: Grimm Center at dawn. | Right: Longitudinal section.

Twelve branch and departmental libraries from the liberal arts and cultural studies as well as social studies and economics were integrated in the new central library, creating the largest contiguous open access library collection in Germany. The central reading reading room is embedded in the open access areas. The work places extend terrace-like over four floors. The whole building is marked by a clear, objective language of form, a sparing use of materials and colors, as well as by a symmetrical ordering. Especially of note is the rigorous extension of the skeleton shaped basic grid throughout the entire building.

From left to right, from above to below:
Extererior view, View into the entrance, Reading terrace with view
to the open-access area, Reading station in the open-access area.
Right: Central reading room.

UNIVERSITY AND STATE LIBRARY OF INNSBRUCK,
INNSBRUCK, AUSTRIA

ECK & REITER ARCHITEKTEN
DIETMAR ROSSMANN ARCHITEKT

www.eck-reiter.at, www.art-zt.at

Client: BIG - Bundesimmobiliengesellschaft mbh, **Completion:** 2009, **Gross floor area:** 4,200 m², **Photos:** Lukas Schaller (108, 110 a. r., 110 b.), Günter Richard Wett (110 a. l., 111).

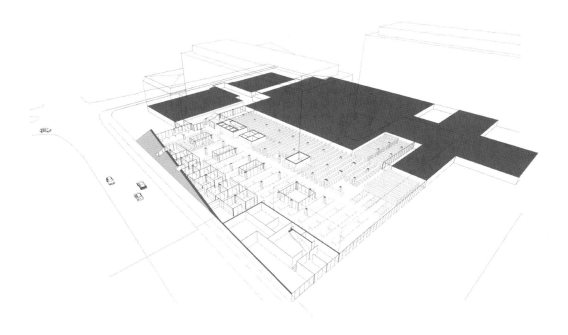

Left: Entrance area of the library. | Right: Axonometry.

With its 4,200 square meters the University and State Library of Innsbruck is the largest scientific library in western Austria. A simple slab which also serves as a roof unifies the book collections of the individual institutions in a faculty library, connecting it with the Neo-Baroque main library. At the same time it operates as a new entrance to the entire grounds and opens the building to the urban surroundings. There are several openings in the slab which admit daylight into the spaces. The atriums which are thereby created were glazed and creatively designed. The work places are grouped together in the center, framed by the book collection and the employee areas.

From left to right, from above to below:
Stairs with atrium, View of the atrium, Atrium, Reading area.
Right: Interior view of the library.

LIBRARY FOR THE FACULTY OF PHILOLOGY,
BERLIN, GERMANY

FOSTER + PARTNERS

www.fosterandpartners.com

Client: Senatsverwaltung fur Stadtentwicklung, **Completion:** 2005, **Gross floor area:** 6,290 m², **Photos:** Nigel Young, Foster + Partners (112, 114 a. r., 114 b. r.), Rudi Meisel (114 a. l., 114 b. l., 115).

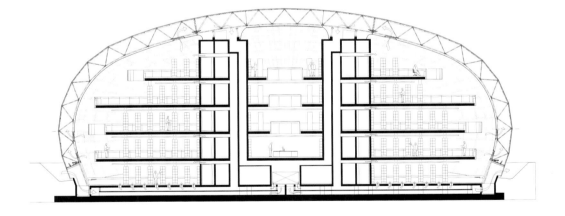

Left: Exterior view at night. | Right: Section.

The new library for the Faculty of Philology lies hidden behind university buildings, encompassing an area of six former courtyards. The bubble-like enclosure, which is clad in aluminium and glazed panels, is supported on steel frames with a radial geometry and contains four floors. An inner membrane of translucent glass fibre filters the daylight and creates an atmosphere of concentration, while scattered transparent openings allow momentary views of the sky and glimpses of sunlight. The bookstacks are located at the center of each floor, with reading desks arranged around the perimeter. The serpentine profile of the floors creates an edge pattern in which each floor swells or recedes with respect to the one above or below it.

From left to right, from above to below:
Left: Reception area, Interior view of the roof,
Reading desks arranged around the perimeter, Reading desks.
Right: View to lower floors.

INGLESIDE BRANCH LIBRARY,
SAN FRANCISCO (CA), USA

FOUGERON ARCHITECTURE

www.fougeron.com

Client: San Francisco Public Library, **Completion:** 2009, **Gross floor area:** 550 m², **Photos:** Joe Fletcher.

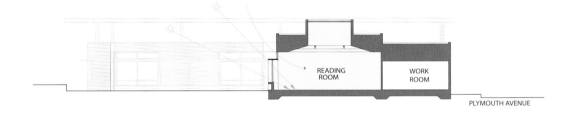

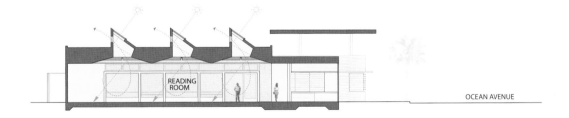

Left: Exterior perspective at night. | Right: Sections, illustrating lighting and ventilation.

The L-shaped scheme allows the main reading room and community room volumes to flank and define a central courtyard. The most striking element of the façade is an egg-shaped children's reading room with a large window that puts its user's activities on display. In the main reading room, floor to ceiling books line the walls. The sloped ceiling of the space is capped with giant skylights coaxing sunlight deep into the room. Facing the courtyard, mahogany-clad carrels offer quiet, intimate spaces to read and relax. Benches are built into the glass edges creating a simple and elegant relationship between courtyard and interior spaces.

Left: Exterior view from Ocean Avenue.

From left to right, from above to below:
Interior courtyard and garden, Main entry with
sun screen and oculus, Teen Room and Connecting Axis
from Main Reading Room.
Right: Main Reading Room with skylight.

SCHOLAR'S LIBRARY,
OLIVE BRIDGE (NY), USA

www.gluckpartners.com

Client: Professor Carol Gluck, **Completion:** 2003, **Gross floor area:** 75 m², **Photos:** Paul Warchol.

Left: Exterior perspective. | Right: Section.

A pure and elegant Platonic cube matches the unity of the building's purpose and form, in both programmatic and metaphorical terms. The first floor is completely closed and contains stacks for books. The second floor, entirely open, is a scholar's working study. The exterior expresses this dual character, with the floating roof cantilevered off the second floor to highlight the distinction between the solid and the void. The windows open on all four sides to create the feeling of an aerie in the woods. The changing seasons provide the context, with the study "walls" green in the summer, orange in the fall, and white in the winter. The study is a serene and solitary haven for quiet work that is at the same time immersed in the natural world around it.

From left to right, from above to below:
Closed windows, Opened windows, Staircase to the upper floor,
View from inside in fall.
Right: Detail of open windows.

TOWN HALL EXTENSION, NEW LIBRARY,
HEERHUGOWAARD, THE NETHERLANDS

www.heeswijk.nl

Client: Municipality of Heerhugowaard, **Completion:** 2006, **Gross floor area:** 19,000 m², **Photos:** Hans van Heeswijk architects (126, 128 a. l.), Luuk Kramer (128 a. r., 128 b., 129).

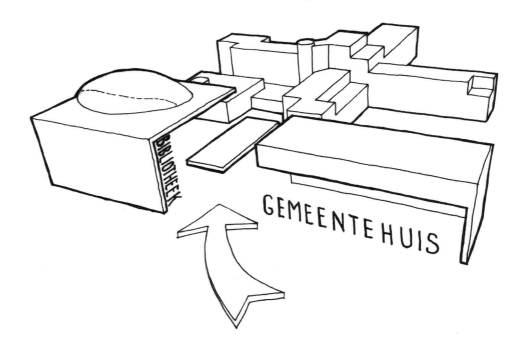

Left: Exterior view of the library and the townhall. | Right: Concept sketch.

The center of Heerhugowaard is changing dramatically. The reason is a new city plaza next to the Town Hall. A new wing of the Town Hall with information and social services for the public opens up the building to the outside world and invites it to come inside. The existing brick buildings are joined by a municipal department, clad in bluestone and a library with a wooden exterior. The nine meter high entrance hall provides spatial coherence. A walkway around the adjacent courtyard connects the existing cube of the meeting hall with the new free-form spaces containing service counters, the book library with cafés, the art lending library and the wedding room. A cupola topped with a mezzanine offers a splendid view of this new heart of Heerhugowaard.

From left to right, from above to below:
Exterior view of the entrance, Entrance area, Reception desk,
Interior view of the library.
Right: Interior of the library.

LIBRARY HTW DRESDEN,
DRESDEN, GERMANY

REIMAR HERBST/ANGELIKA KUNKLER www.reimarherbstarchitekten.de

Client: Freistaat Sachsen, **Completion:** 2006, **Gross floor area:** 3,933 m², **Photos:** Lothar Sprenger.

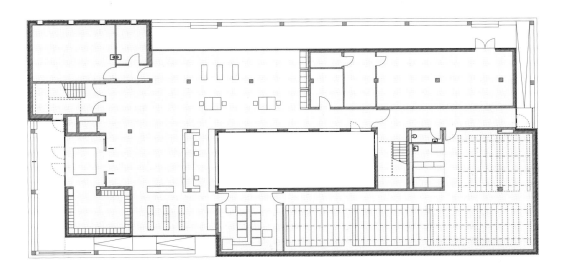

Left: View over the place to the library. | Right: Ground floor plan.

As the intellectual center of the College of Technology and Economics the new library connects the adjacent college building to a spatially interwoven ensemble. With its height and width it extends the volume of an adjacent building. The book collections and reading areas are located in three upper floors over the entry way of the library. The building surrounds the atrium, to which all the library areas are oriented. The reading places are located on the façades facing the sun and the atrium. The façades evince the typology of a book case: Deep narrow window openings with flush oak windows make for a strikingly profiled exterior façade.

From left to right, from above to below:
Main entrance, View at night from the rose garden, Entrance area,
Natural stone and glass element.
Right: Reading room along the façade.

STATE LIBRARY AT UNTER DEN LINDEN,
BERLIN, GERMANY

HG MERZ ARCHITEKTEN
MUSEUMSGESTALTER

www.hgmerz.com

Client: Stiftung Preußischer Kulturbesitz, **Completion:** 2011 / 2013, **Gross floor area:** 110,000 m², **Photos:** hg merz architekten museumsgestalter (134, 136 b.), Udo Meinel (136 a. l., 136 a. r., 137).

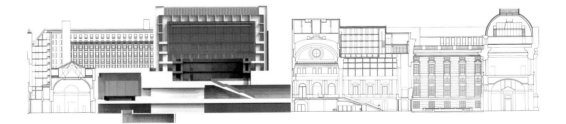

Left: Visualization of the new reading room. | Right: Longitudinal section.

The cupola hall of the State Library was so badly damaged during the Second World War, that the ruins were eventually torn down. The building thereby lost its spiritual and material midpoint. The goal of the building procedure was to give back an architecturally and intellectually rich historical location to the city. The lighting cube of the new building rises up on top of a massive base, assuming the proportions of the old reading room. The axial opening of the building is retained, terminating in the ascent into the new reading room. The luminous cube also sets a distinct tone from outside and without relinquishing any architectural independence fits into the structure of the building.

From left to right, from above to below:
Façade of the new reading room, Detail of new façade,
Visualization of the new reading room with gallery.
Right: Exterior view of the new reading room in the ensemble.

THE REGIONAL LIBRARY OF BIZKAIA,
BILBAO, SPAIN

IMB ARQUITECTOS

www.imbarquitectos.es

Client: Diputación Foral de Bizkaia, Bizkaiko Foru Aldundia, **Completion:** 2007, **Photos:** Courtesy of the architects.

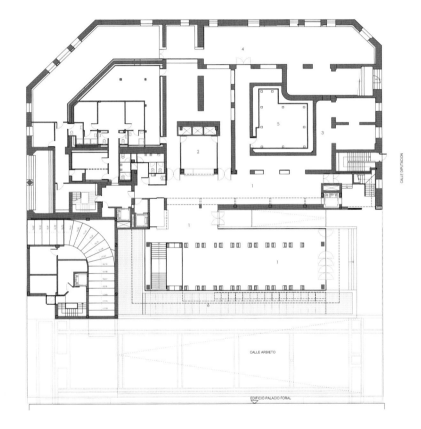

1 HALL. FOYER
2 OFICIAL BULLETINS
3 PUBLICATIONS
4 READING ROOM AND ARCHIVE
5 CLOSED STOREROOM
6 POOL
7 PARKING RAMP

Left: Interior view. | Right: Ground floor plan.

The site includes an existing building, which had to be reformed, and an open space permitting a new construction according to client requirements. The new construction includes two new buildings. The first one, covered with stone, houses the administration. The second one serves to store the books and is designed like a glass container. The texture of the books is used to establish a cultural claim and make evident the dialogue between the interior of the building and the public space in the outside. During the day the image of the printed serigraphies, which represent the written content of the books, is predominating. At night the artificial illumination intensifies the aura of the books stored in the shelves.

From left to right, from above to below:
Water basin at entrance, Exterior view, Lecture room, Interior view
entrance area.
Right: Exterior view at night.

CITY LIBRARY IN TURKU,
TURKU, FINLAND

www.jkmm.fi

Client: Turku City, **Completion:** 2007, **Gross floor area:** 6,900 m², **Photos:** Arno de la Chapelle (142, 144 l., 145), Michael Perlmutter (144 r.).

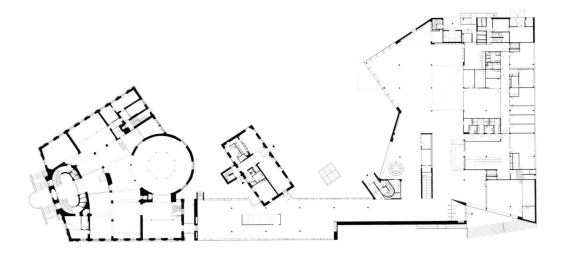

Left: Exterior view from the street. | Right: Ground floor plan.

The new city library in Turku is located at the historical center of the city. The building is the latest addition to a block with several historical buildings. The new main entrance opens onto the corner of two main streets. Public spaces are situated mainly on two floors surrounding the inner courtyard. The main room is reached through a stairway, which opens to a monu-mental space. For the interior, mostly European oak is used in the wall covering and furniture. The façades are mainly plastered. Natural stone is used extensively on the façades, the stairway and the grounds surrounding the building. Glass was also given a seminal role both in the outer architecture and the interior world. Transparency befits this type of building; a public library building should evoke the idea of openness.

From left to right, from above to below:
Entrance area, Exterior view from the inner courtyard, Wooden
furniture in the library, Library.
Right: Main room.

AMSTERDAM PUBLIC LIBRARY,
AMSTERDAM, THE NETHERLANDS

JO COENEN & CO ARCHITEKTEN

www.jocoenen.com
Client: Oosterdokseiland Ontwikkeling & City of Amsterdam, **Completion:** 2007, **Gross floor area:** 28,500 m², **Photos:** Rob Hoekstra (146), Arjen Schmitz (148 a. l., 148 b. r., 149), Luuk Kramer (148 a. r., 148 b. l.).

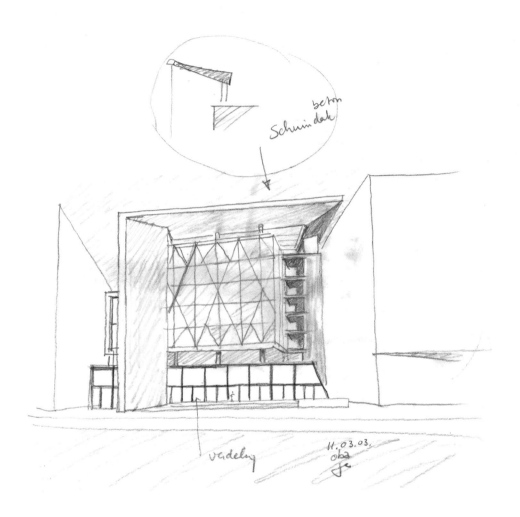

Left: Façade. | Right: Design sketch.

The new city library will be the centerpiece of the Oosterdokseiland, a redeveloped area in Amsterdam. The total built area is 28,500 square meters and is located in an urban envelope with a volume of about 40 meters in height, 40 meters in width and 120 meters in length. The library was designed as an interior meeting place and an easily discernable landmark in the Amsterdam townscape. Form, function and technique are inextricably linked. The materialization of the exterior in natural stone continues in the the interior. The library is one of the three European ECO Buildings and received various awards, among them the WAN Award Public Building of the Year in 2009.

From left to right, from above to below:
Southern façade, View of the atrium,
Reception area, Workstations.
Right: Reading area, Periodicals section.

THE NATIONAL LIBRARY OF BELARUS,
MINSK, BELARUS

MIKHAIL VINOGRADOV, VIKTOR KRAMARENKO

www.kramarenko.com

Client: Executive Committee of the City Minsk, **Completion:** 2005, **Gross floor area:** 113,670 m², **Photos:** Courtesy of the architect.

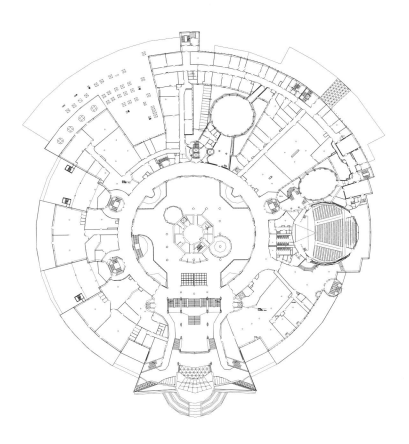

Left: Exterior view. | Right: Ground floor plan.

The new building of the National Library of Belarus is located on the main avenue of the capital. It has the shape of a diamond, placed in the center of the three-storied surrounding stylobate. The main entrance is constructed in the shape of two open book pages which reflect the development of the world and Slavonic writing. The 20 reading rooms of the library are differentiated by materials in accordance with subject and category. They offer 2,000 workstations, equipped with electronic circulation desks, scanning, copying and printing devices. All reading rooms are light and comfortable, giving a view on the riverside and the park area. The uniqueness of the library is its book stack, which is located in the high-rise part of the building.

From left to right, from above to below:
Main entrance, Night illumination, Detail of façade,
Interior view of main atrium.
Right: Main atrium.

LIBRARY, MEDIA CENTER AND ARCHIVE,
KREMS, AUSTRIA

ARCHITEKTUR KRAMMER

www.architektur-krammer.at

Client: City of Krems an der Donau, **Completion:** 2008, **Gross floor area:** 435 m², **Photos:** Andreas Buchberger/Wien.

Left: Reception desk. | Right: Elevation reception desk and library.

In 2009 the library and Media Center was relocated to the western wing of the former Krems Dominican monastery, which goes back to the 13th century. Crucial for the conversion plans from the art historical point of view was the Baroque phases around 1730/1740. The goal in the interior was to display the 18th century spacial shell. After the discovery of mu-

ral paintings and painted inscriptions the architects decided to expose to view a portion of the architectural history in the reception room of the first floor. The new library stretches out over 435 square meters. 31,000 books, 720 magazines and almost 4,000 audio visual media are at the disposal of the reading public. Access to the city archive and the scientific library fill out the extensive offer of information.

From left to right, from above to below:
Exterior view of the former cloister, Baroque façade, View to the
children's library, Interior view.
Right: Reading area.

NATIONAL LIBRARY OF CHINA,
BEIJING, CHINA

KSP JÜRGEN ENGEL ARCHITEKTEN

www.ksp-architekten.de

Client: National Library of China, **Completion:** 2008, **Gross floor area:** 80,000 m², **Photos:** Hans Schlupp.

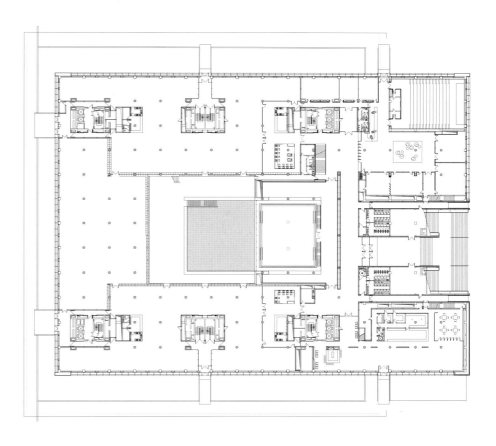

Left: Exterior view at night. | Right: Ground floor plan.

The task is to extend the existing library by 80,000 square meters in order to accommodate approximately twelve million books. The design contribution of KSP Jürgen Engel Architekten is divided into three main areas: the raised pedestal, the library in the classical sense of the historical "Si Ku Quan Shu" collection, representing the past, columns, creat-ing a zone for interaction of the people with their historical heritage, representing the present, and the floating roof, the "Digital Library", that stands for the future. The three areas are also stylistic elements of the Chinese building history mainly reserved for official buildings. The design consciously takes up these elements in the form of a contemporary interpretation.

From left to right, from above to below:
Side view, Detail of the façade, Interior view ground floor,
Detail of window.
Right: Interior view.

LOHJA MAIN LIBRARY,
LOHJA, FINLAND

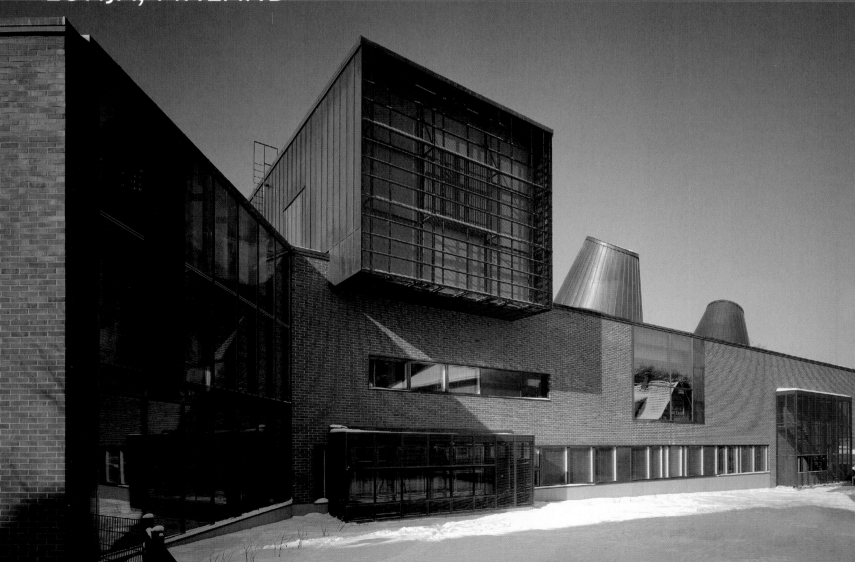

LAHDELMA & MAHLAMÄKI

www.arklm.fi
Client: City of Lohja, **Completion:** 2005, **Gross floor area:** 3,513 m², **Photos:** Jussi Tiainen.

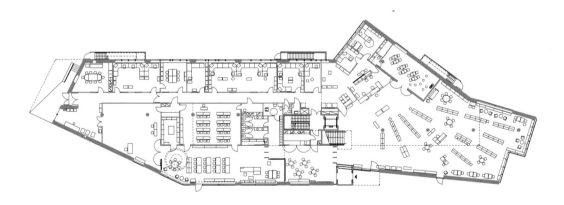

Left: Exterior view. | Right: Ground floor plan.

The Lohja Main Library is the result of an open competition which the architects won in 2002. The new building is harmoniously integrated into the cultural campus area, within the Church Saint Laurentius, the Hall of Laurentius, the Music Academy of Länsi-Uusimaa and the Academy of Hiisi. Due to the proximity of the old church, the library building was kept low. The functions of the building are divided in two floors. The public spaces in the first floor are spaciously widened with the help of different sized skylights. The long walls of the building are of red brick. The inner spaces open through the gables towards the church and the center. Proverbs from the Lohja area are silk printed on the glass of these openings.

From left to right, from above to below:
Entrance, Glazed façade at night, Main view, Interior staircase.
Right: Interior of the library.

CHILDREN'S TOY LIBRARY,
BONNEUIL-SUR-MARNE, FRANCE

LAN ARCHITECTURE

www.lan-paris.com
Client: Bonneuil-sur-Marne Local Authority, **Completion:** 2008, **Gross floor area:** 380 m², **Photos:** Jean Marie Monthiers.

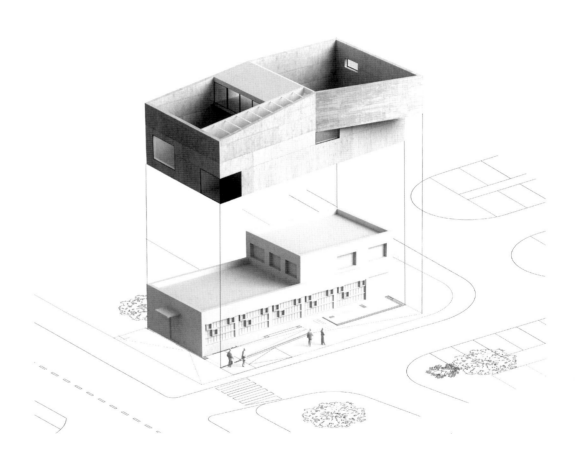

Left: Exterior view. | Right: 3D-model.

The Bonneuil-sur-Marne children's toy library is a public building as well as a play space for children. It is located in an area where 1960's social housing has had a strong physical and social impact. The architects wanted to create a strong urban symbol able to stand out from its environment, whose shell would protect its core. The architects designed a building that appears timeless, an urban symbol standing out from its environment, as a shell able to protect its contents. The monolithic elevations are closely linked to the surrounding urban context. The result is a bunker-like volume that seems always to have been there.

From left to right, from above to below:
Glazed edge of the building, Interior courtyard, View to interior
courtyard, Skylights.
Right: Main playing area.

BASELLAND CANTON LIBRARY,
LIESTAL, SWITZERLAND

LIECHTI GRAF ZUMSTEG ARCHITEKTEN

www.lgz.ch

Client: Baselland Canton, **Completion:** 2005, **Gross floor area:** 4,211 m², **Photos:** Rötheli / Schultz, Baden.

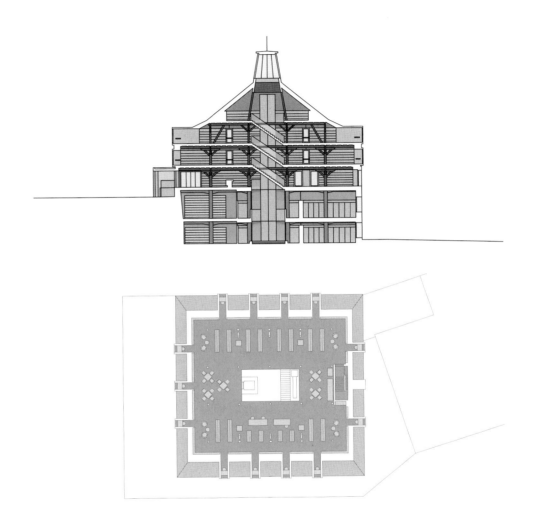

Left: Exterior view. | Right: Section and floor plan first floor.

The wine warehouse built in 1924 was rebuilt in such a way that allowed old and new to fuse inseparably into a whole. The original appearance of the building provides a departure point to find a new form, which would be inconceivable without the existing structure. The clay tile covered roof became a cubic, iconic body seated on the plinth. A lantern exaggerates this striking roof shape. The glazed atrium with stairs and elevators in the interior constitute the center of the library. Dominated by the original massive wooden support structure the rooms are surrounded by bookshelves with window insets serving as reading niches.

From left to right, from above to below:
North façade, "Lantern", Reflecting Pool in the atrium,
Reading niche.
Right: Atrium with main staircase.

ESPAÑA LIBRARY,
MEDELLÍN, COLOMBIA

MAZZANTI & ARQUITECTOS S.A.

www.giancarlomazzanti.com

Client: Alcaldia de Medellin, **Completion:** 2007, **Gross floor area:** 3,727 m², **Photos:** Sergio Gomez (174, 176 a. l., 176 b., 177), Carlos Tobon (176 a. r.).

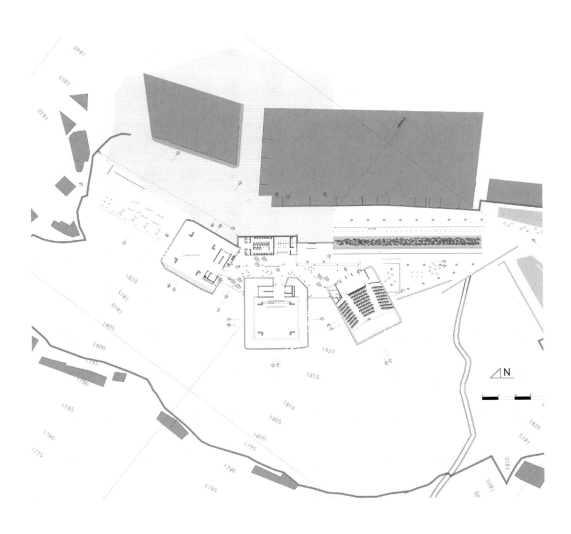

Left: Library above the city. | Right: Ground floor plan.

The España Library is noticeable from much of the city, allowing it to define itself as the symbol of a new Medellín. It stands up like a rock, making itself part of the topography. The first premise of the architects was to develop a building that could de-contextualize the individual from the poverty that surrounds him, by creating a warm atmosphere based on natural light. The building takes a timid look into the city through small windows in the stone-clad façade that show the relation with the valley, letting light enter mainly from the top of the building. The architects divide the required program containing a library, training rooms, and auditorium in three single units which are connected by a plat-form on the first floor.

From left to right, from above to below:
Library like rocks, Bird's eye view, Reading room,
Detail of windows.
Right: View.

DEUSTO UNIVERSITY LIBRARY,
BILBAO, SPAIN

Client: Deusto University, **Completion:** 2009, **Gross floor area:** 25,000 m², **Photos:** Roland Halbe / artur.

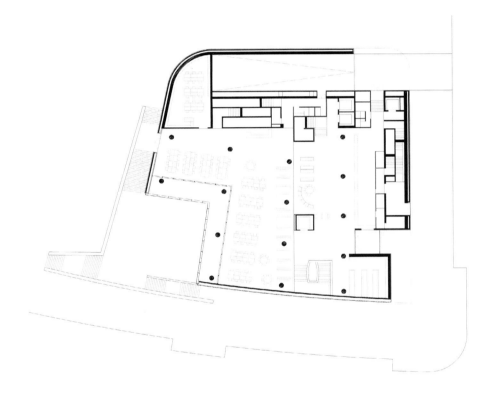

Left: Exterior perspective. | Right: Ground floor plan.

On the one hand the new library building should not compete in any way with the well-deserved promi-nence of the Guggenheim Bilbao, while on the other hand the new building had to express its public nature and establish as much as possible continuity with the University. The glass block allows for a neutral, monolithic and monochromatic volume that does not compete with the shine of the Guggenheim and that is capable of integrating itself with the green universe of the park. Perhaps the building's most salient architec-tural feature is the rounded corners that make it ap-pear to be an independent and autonomous solid. The architect wants the building to be seen as just one more element in the park, which becomes evident in the positioning of the patio.

From left to right, from above to below:
Detail of entrance, Exterior view at night, Reading room with view.
Right: Reading room.

BUCERIUS LAW SCHOOL LIBRARY,
HAMBURG, GERMANY

MEDING PLAN + PROJEKT GMBH

www.mpp.de

Client: Ebelin and Gerd Bucerius ZEIT Foundation, **Completion:** 2007, **Gross floor area:** 4,500 m², **Photos:** Ralf Buscher, Hamburg.

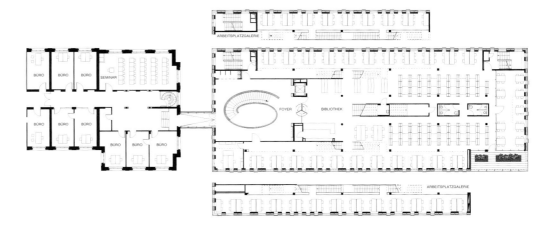

Left: View of the library over the campus. | Right: First floor plan library.

The newly constructed library was build as an extension of the existing main building, drawing attention to the interface between urbane city structure and the historical park. The glass façade lends the building an independent character, while the color design orients to the main building, contributing to a harmony between traditional and contemporary architecture. The vertical arrangement of the colored glass panels resembles the myriad book spines of a book shelf, signalling the intended use of the new building. At three locations on the façade two story, glazed winter gardens were created which the students use as meeting points and chilling out areas.

From left to right, from above to below:
Detail façade, Aerial view of the campus, Interior view of the foyer,
Staircase in the library.
Right: Workstations.

BOOK MOUNTAIN,
SPIJKENISSE, THE NETHERLANDS

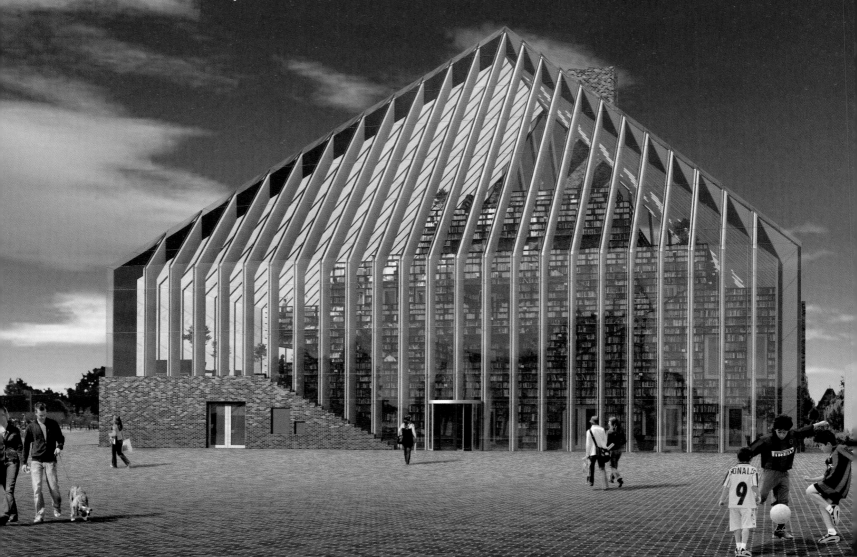

MVRDV

www.mvrdv.nl

Client: Municipality of Spijkenisse, The Netherlands, **Completion:** 2011, **Gross floor area:** 10,000 m², **Photos:** MVRDV, Rotterdam.

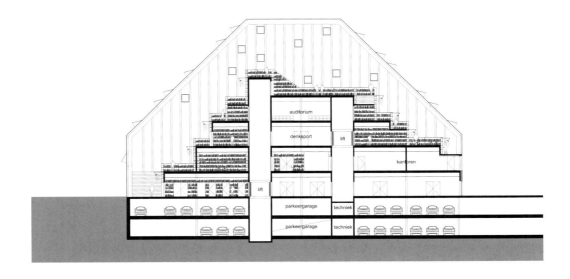

Left: The exterior shape refers to Dutch barn style. | Right: Longitudinal section.

The new public library will be located in the inner city of Spijkenisse. The shape and material of the building refer to a traditional Dutch barn style typology; as a memento to the agricultural history of Spijkenisse Village. By stacking facilities such as offices, meeting rooms and auditorium vertically, terraces of different sizes emerge upon which the book shelves are positioned, creating a grand book mountain. The terraces are linked by staircases that curve around the mountain to the top. The book mountain is covered by a glass shell, creating a bell jar, an open-air library. Solar protection, natural ventilation and an underground heat storage system provide for comfortable conditions all year round. The climate system is a carefully balanced collection of sustainable features.

From left to right, from above to below:
On the top a panoramic view of Spijkenisse awaits, A route connecting the terraces and reading areas curves up.
Right: Terraces of different sizes emerge upon which the
book shelves are positioned.

UNIVERSITY OF POZNAN LIBRARY,
POZNAN, POLAND

CONSULTOR / APA BULAT / NEOSTUDIO ARCHITECTS

www.neostudioweb.eu

Client: Adam Mickiewicz University Poznan, **Completion:** 2009, **Gross floor area:** 2,062 m², **Photos:** Pawel Swierowski / neostudio architects.

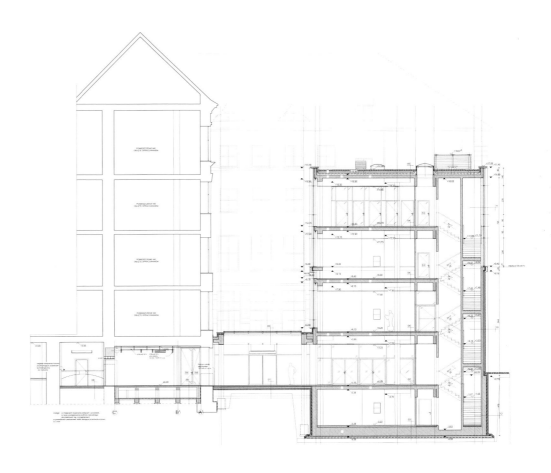

Left: Exterior perspective. | Right: Section.

The library is located in the heart of Poznan – in close proximity to historical buildings from the beginning of 20th century. The parcel is bordered on three sides by the Collegium Maius and by the building of Regional Government Office. The building's structure is halved horizontally with a massive sandstone bottom and a light glass top – to represent a merger of historical content with a very contemporary form. The building's façades are dominated by glass and sandstone. The used stone pattern is identical to the existing one at the façades of Collegium Maius facility. At the same time some light rhythmic disturbances were introduced, by the sandstone forms that appear throughout the entire building elevations and that are also further reflected in the interior.

From left to right, from above to below:
View from the main street, Library in context, Entrance hall.
Right: Reading room with a view.

FLEET LIBRARY AT THE RHODE ISLAND SCHOOL OF DESIGN,
PROVIDENCE (RI), USA

OFFICE DA

www.officeda.com

Client: Rhode Island School of Design, **Completion:** 2006, **Gross floor area:** 5,100 m², **Photos:** John Horner Photography.

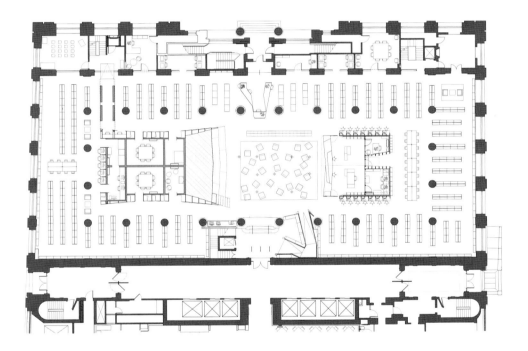

Left: View from the study island with reading area. | Right: Ground floor plan.

The approach for the RISD library employed not one, but three distinct architectural tactics: preservation, engineering, and architectural intervention. The library is located in the main hall of the historic Hospital Trust Bank building. It houses an extensive collection of art and design volumes, magazines, and multi-media resources, as well as group study areas, classrooms, and administrative offices. Two new pavilions housing key programmatic components were positioned within the barrel vaulted void of the main hall. The negotiation between the purity of the architecture in the space, and the insertion of new elements defines a strategy of camouflage as a way of threading new elements into the space as inconspicuously as possible.

From left to right, from above to below:
View from the study island to the lounge, Detail of stairs to the
study island, Reading booths underneath the study island,
Bird's eye view of the library.
Right: View of the library.

CHONGQING LIBRARY,
CHONGQING, CHINA

PERKINS EASTMAN

www.perkinseastman.com

Client: Chongqing Land Property Group, **Completion:** 2007, **Gross floor area:** 50,100 m², **Photos:** Tim Griffith (198), ZhiHui Gu (200, 201).

Left: Main entrance. | Right: Axonometry.

The new Chongqing Library is an urban complex that respects the long and unique culture of its predecessor while projecting a modern image. The program exemplifies the library's transformation from a repository for books into a cultural center which in addition to an exhibition hall, also houses computer learning facilities, ancient archives, and reading rooms, not to mention hotel rooms, a public theater, a conferencing center, and a restaurant. The design concept was predicated on the notion that learning, knowledge, and the exchange of ideas must be free, open, and accessible to all. The building is sheathed almost entirely in glass, inscribed with a text pattern of selected quotes that serve as a reminder of the profound life-long impact of learning.

中文期刊阅览区
中文报纸阅览区 Chinese Newspaper Reading Area →

From left to right, from above to below:
View across the south pool, Atrium, Periodical Reading Room.
Right: Reading room.

NATIONAL TECHNICAL LIBRARY,
PRAGUE, CZECH REPUBLIC

PROJEKTIL ARCHITEKTI

www.projektil.cz

Client: Státní technická knihovna, Ministerstvo školství, mládeže a tělovýchovy, **Completion:** 2009, **Gross floor area:** 51,434 m², **Photos:** Andrea Lhotáková.

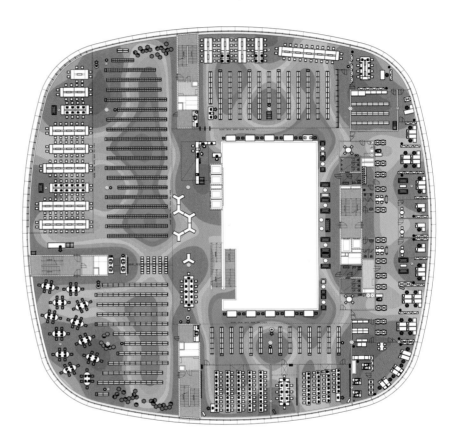

Left: Exterior view. | Right: Floor plan second floor.

This project is the architects' answer to the role of the library in today's society. The building should be urban developmentally important and environmentally friendly. The ground floor houses public spaces like the cafe, exhibition hall, bookshop, cloak room and night study room. The entry to the library is right in the middle of the atrium. The actual library occupies the upper four floors. Part of the concept is the surrounding area – social spaces on the west and a green park on the east. Finally, the building was designed including the interior. Art and the graphic design follow the concept "the technological schoolbook", so that illustrations are deliberately shown to better understand the building's design and functions.

From left to right, from above to below:
Lobby, Main hall library, Reading room.
Right: Main hall library.

RESEARCH LIBRARY,
HRADEC KRÁLOVÉ, CZECH REPUBLIC

PROJEKTIL ARCHITEKTI

www.projektil.cz

Client: Studijní a vědecká knihovna v Hradci Králové, Ministerstvo kultury ČR, **Completion:** 2008, **Gross floor area:** 2,920 m², **Photos:** Andrea Lhotáková.

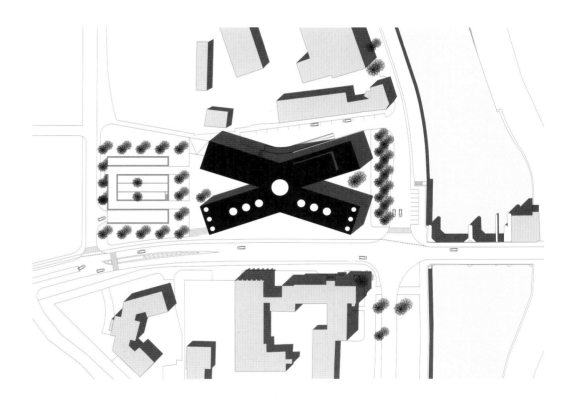

Left: Exterior view from the street. | Right: Site plan.

The five-story building consists of a concrete construction also visible in the monolithic fair faced concrete façade. The building is shaped like an "X". The main vertical component, illuminated by a circular roof light is located in the center of the X. The distribution of visitors, librarians and books takes place from the central vertical point to the four wings of the X. The library space with bookshelves and study rooms is located in the two eastern wings and occupies three floors. In the other wings there are offices, storage and a conference hall. The interior atmosphere is created by fair faced concrete walls and ceilings, colored floors and wooden accents. An important part of the building design is the energy-saving concept.

From left to right, from above to below:
Detail of the façade, Exterior view, Library, View of the staircase.
Right: Study room in the library.

BLOOR / GLADSTONE BRANCH LIBRARY,
TORONTO, CANADA

RDH ARCHITECTS INC.

www.rdharch.com
Client: The Toronto Public Library, **Completion:** 2009, **Gross floor area:** 1,950 m², **Photos:** Bloor/Gladstone Branch, Toronto Public Library.

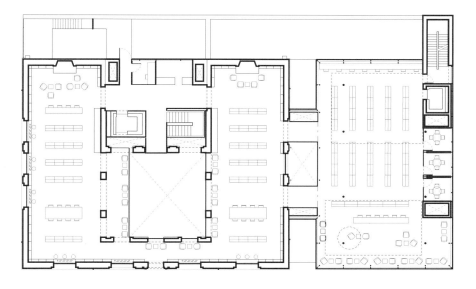

Left: North elevation. | Right: Main level floor plan.

The Bloor/Gladstone Branch library is a renovation and addition to a listed heritage library in downtown Toronto. The architects were commissioned to design an additional 900 square meters, bringing the facilities to a level consistent with a district library. This project transforms an outdated heritage facility into a functioning, interactive, contemporary library.

The level of finish, detail and design resolution elevates the library to a level commensurate with other significant cultural institutions, a level which illustrates the fundamental importance of access to information and public spaces in the world's largest library system, the Toronto Public Library.

From left to right, from above to below:
North-west corner with elevated reading atrium, Connection to
existing façade, Staircase, Glass elevator and staff check point.
Right: Main collection space with reading atrium.

ROLEX LEARNING CENTER,
LAUSANNE, SWITZERLAND

SANAA

www.sanaa.co.jp

Client: EPFL, **Completion:** 2009, **Gross floor area:** 20,000 m², **Photos:** EPFL & Hisao Suzuki (214, 216 a., 216 b. l., 217), EPFL Alain Herzog (216 b. r.).

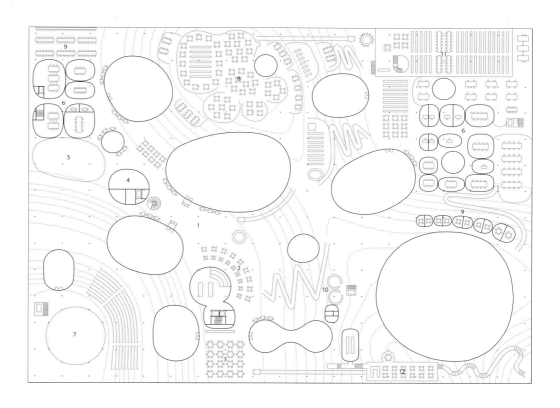

Left: Bird's eye view of Rolex Learning Center. | Right: Floor plan second floor.

The main library, containing 500,000 printed works, is one of the largest scientific collections in Europe. Four large study areas can accommodate 860 students with office space for over 100 employees; a state-of-the-art multimedia library will give access to 10,000 online journals and 17,000 e-books, with advanced check out machines and systems for bibliographic search. A study center for use by postgraduate researchers will provide access to the university's major archive and research collection, and there are teaching areas including 10 "bubbles" for seminars, group work and other meetings. All main sections are separated without walls, demarcated instead by the inner landscape of a large open space.

From left to right, from above to below:
Southern arch with restaurant, Promenade inside,
Work spaces in the library.
Right: Rolex Learning Center at night.

HALMSTAD LIBRARY,
HALMSTAD, SWEDEN

SCHMIDT HAMMER LASSEN
ARCHITECTS

www.shl.dk

Client: The Municipality of Halmstad, **Completion:** 2006, **Gross floor area:** 8,000 m², **Photos:** schmidt hammer lassen architects.

Left: View across the Nissan. | Right: Ground floor plan.

Halmstad Library is set within a park next to the Nissan River. The atrium encircling a large existing chestnut tree becomes its fulcrum, with the long concave façade with double-height glazing suspended between the seemingly floating floor-plates. Nature, seasons and the city, all become part of the library. Inside, the library is essentially a single open space, flexible and highly legible: an open structure which allows an active interplay between the columns and the trees outside. The library is constructed of few and simple materials: concrete, glass and Nordic larch flooring. The Library is raised above street level on a forest of columns echoing the trees surrounding the building.

From left to right, from above to below:
View towards the Nissan, View along the façade from inside,
Double height library space, Trees are part of the interior.
Right: Entrance.

URBAN MEDIASPACE,
AARHUS, DENMARK

SCHMIDT HAMMER LASSEN
ARCHITECTS

www.shl.dk

Client: The Municipality of Aarhus and Realdania, **Completion:** 2014, **Gross floor area:** 30,000 m², **Photos:** schmidt hammer lassen architects.

Left: View from the plaza in front of the building. | Right: Situation.

Urban Mediaspace will be Scandinavia's largest public library and represents a new generation of modern hybrid libraries. Urban Mediaspace is part of the ambitious district plan to revitalise the former industrial cargo docks on the harbor front by connecting the area to the historic center of the city. The main concept is a covered urban space. A large heptagonal slice hovers above a glazed prism, which is resting on a square of snow flake-shaped stairs fanning out to the edge of the sea. The heptagon will contain the media house administration and offices for rent. The glass building below is transparent and allows passers-by visual access to the activities in the library while the users have a 360 degree panoramic view from the inside.

HERZOGIN ANNA AMALIA LIBRARY – STUDY CENTER,
WEIMAR, GERMANY

KARL-HEINZ SCHMITZ AND
HILDE BARZ-MALFATTI

www.schmitz-architekt.de

Client: Klassik Stiftung Weimar, **Completion:** 2005, **Gross floor area:** 14,214 m², **Photos:** Ulrich Schwarz.

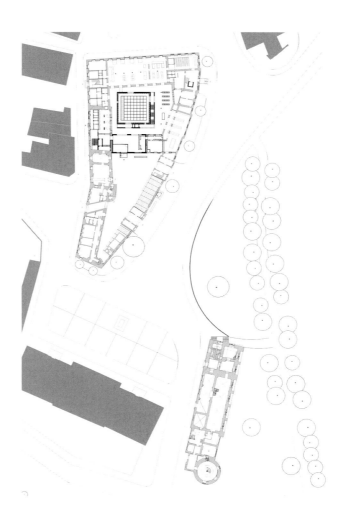

Left: Interior view of the library. | Right: Ground floor plan.

A complex of six buildings, ranging from the early Renaissance to the early 20th century was augmented by a new entry building, a book cube and by underground magazines housing approximately one million books. These underground spaces link the New Study center with the old library which is situated on the other side of the square. The cubic book-space, which was inserted in the old courtyard, constitutes the core of the new facility and establishes a quiet center within a heterogeneous floor plan. The interior of this space is reminiscent of the rococo hall of the Duchess Anna Amalia Library. The public and administrative areas of the new study center are distributed around the book cube on several levels.

From left to right, from above to below:
New entrance building, View to the entrance, New staircase,
Book cube.
Right: Reading room.

VIANA DO CASTELO LIBRARY,
VIANA DO CASTELO, PORTUGAL

ÁLVARO SIZA

www.alvarosizavieira.com

Client: Municipality of Viana do Castelo, **Completion:** 2008, **Gross floor area:** 3,077 m², **Photos:** FG + SG - Fotografia de Arquitectura.

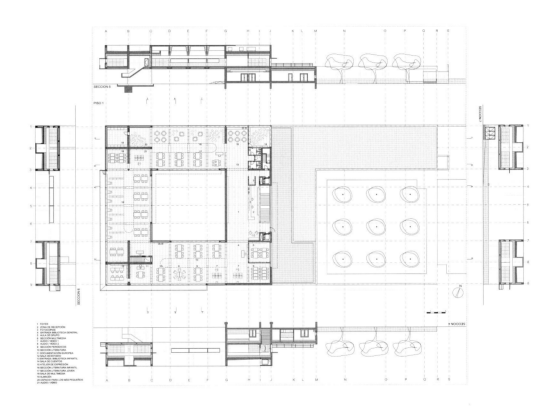

Left: View from the river. | Right: First floor plan.

The library sits on the L-shaped ground floor and consists of a raised square. It has a volume of 45 x 45 meters, defining an inner courtyard of 20 x 20 meters. In order that the landscape can flow continuously, this large volume should not disturb the view to the river from the street and the surroundings. The architect ensures the view of the river by this elevated construction and creates framed views on the street level, with a large riverside inner garden. The ground floor hosts the entrance, offices, conference rooms and archives, while the actual library is on the first floor, additionally lit by skylights. The façade consists of exposed white concrete, while the natural stone cladding of the building base is in dialogue with the surrounding nature.

From left to right, from above to below:
The elevated first floor frames the view towards the river, View towards the city, Interior on ground floor.
Right: Library on the first floor with skylights.

BEEC – HISTORICAL ARCHIVE AND LIBRARY,
PALERMO, ITALY

STUDIO ITALO ROTA & PARTNERS

www.studioitalorota.it

Client: Sicilian Regional Assembly, **Completion:** 2007, **Gross floor area:** 300 m², **Photos:** Giovanni Chiara-monte.

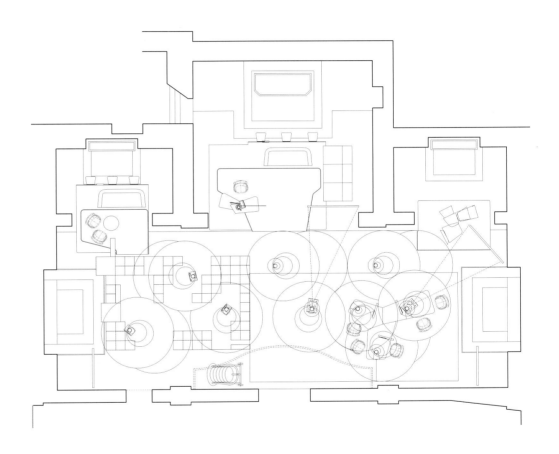

Left: Detail of book case. | Right: Floor plan.

The Sant'Elena and Costantino Oratory that flanks the Palazzo dei Normanni in Palermo, was constructed at the end of the 16th century. In the past it served as the center of Confraternita of Madonna di Monserrato, the religious cult imported from Spain. The interior design of the library is that of a grand installation in a restored space. The project retains the structure of the old building and tries to preserve the original atmosphere so that the future users breathe a certain spirituality. The architects have proposed a different utilisation of the existing space, not a simple re-use of the old building. Finally the project succeeds by interpreting Palermo's culture and architecture's "variety" and by its ability to fascinate anyone who gets close to it.

From left to right, from above to below:
Reading area with mushrooms-columns and, Bookshelf, Detail of
bookshelf bookcase with glass case.
Right: View to the ceiling.

SANDRO PENNA MEDIATHEQUE-LIBRARY,
PERUGIA, ITALY

STUDIO ITALO ROTA

www.studioitalorota.it

Client: Municipality of Perugia, **Completion:** 2004, **Gross floor area:** 800 m², **Photos:** Tomas Clocchiatti.

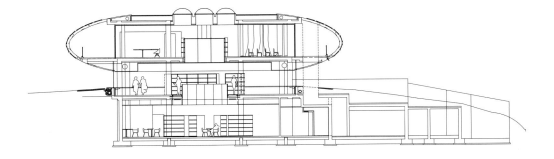

Left: Exterior view. | Right: Section.

The building exploits the natural profile of the land from which it partly emerges, giving the impression of a great disk having landed in the town. The original vegetation has been maintained with passages cut through the current embankment. In this area we find the large illuminated windows, with blow-ups of pages from books, which can be regularly updated, forming a great luminous book. From the gallery it is possible to see the whole central space, up to the porthole-shaped skylights which illuminate the heart of the building. Natural light filtered through the large pink-tinted windows is exploited as much as possible. This creates a relaxing atmosphere which favours concentration, which is also aided by the zenithal light of the skylights.

From left to right, from above to below:
Detail of illuminated screens, Detail of roof cover, Interior view,
Reading room second floor.
Right: Library at second floor.

UNIVERSITY LIBRARY OF THE UNIVERSITY OF AMSTERDAM,
AMSTERDAM, THE NETHERLANDS

BUREAU IRA KOERS & STUDIO ROELOF MULDER

www.roelofmulder.com, www.irakoers.nl

Client: University of Amsterdam, **Completion:** 2009, **Gross floor area:** 2,300 m², **Photos:** roelof mulder & ira koers.

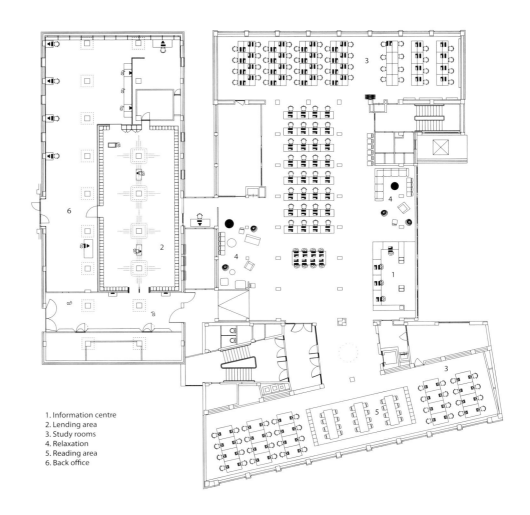

1. Information centre
2. Lending area
3. Study rooms
4. Relaxation
5. Reading area
6. Back office

Left: Lending area. | Right: Floor plan.

A library has been turned into a "home" in which to study. A growing number of students, between 1,500 and 5,000 every day, visit the University Library in order to study and pick up their digitally ordered books. Despite future plans for a new building, the university wished to have a new, temporary interior design for the 2,500 square meter space that would comprise study rooms plus 235 extra workplaces, a canteen, the information center and an automated check out area. The designers wanted to achieve a space like a white page of a book, in which the students themselves would play the main role. In red cabinets with 1,105 red crates, piles of books wait for their borrowers. This is the heart of the University Library.

From left to right, from above to below:
Telephone area in the hallway, Reading area, Information desk,
Entrance to lending section.
Right: Relaxation corner in the main study room.

LIBRARY IN PROVILLE,
PROVILLE, FRANCE

TANK ARCHITECTES

www.tank.fr

Client: Town of Proville, **Completion:** 2008, **Gross floor area:** 610 m^2, **Photos:** Julien Lanoo.

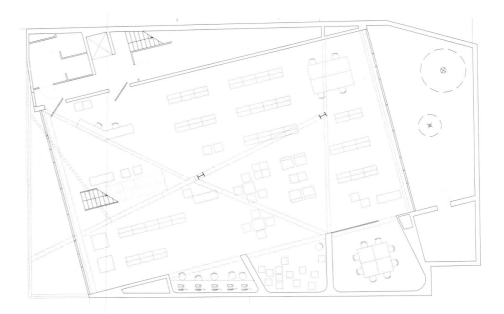

Left: Exterior view. | Right: Ground floor plan.

The new mediatheque of Proville opens onto the village and becomes a place of exchange and culture, a public library and a surprising and enthusiastic place inviting everyone to the pleasure of reading. The idea was to create a contemporary building dealing with the environment and the existing elements. The mediatheque has a metallic frame clad in wood that will turn grey as it ages. Large aluminium windows lets in lots of natural light to get into the building, allowing the users of the library to communicate with the town. The roof, overlooking the church tower and the trees, can be used as a terrace for reading outdoors.

From left to right, from above to below:
Roof of the library, View from the roof inside at night, Interior of
the library, Office space.
Right: Library with relaxation area.

LANGARA COLLEGE LIBRARY,
VANCOUVER, CANADA

TEEPLE ARCHITECTS

www.teeplearch.com
Client: Langara College, **Completion:** 2007, **Gross floor area:** 7,400 m², **Photos:** Shai Gil Photography.

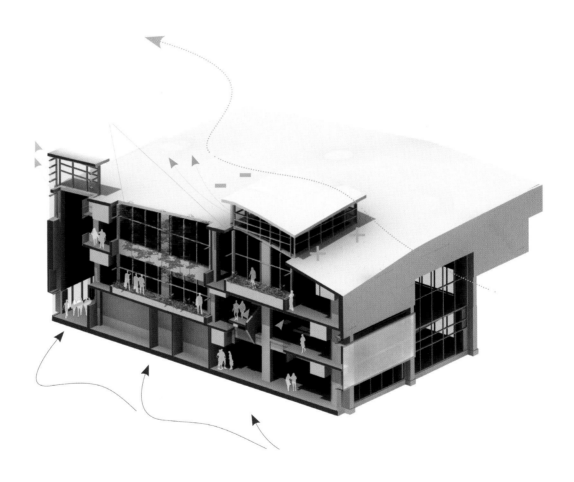

Left: Front Elevatin. | Right: Section with wind tower.

Located in Vancouver, B.C., the approx. 7,500 square meter building program includes a library, multiple classrooms, computational labs, study lounges and faculty offices. The design approach considers both formal and environmental issues. The appearance, program and ecological features of the building are so intermingled that they are indistinguishable. Fresh air is brought into the building through a wind-scoop that becomes an iconic element in the adjacent student quad. The primary building material is local recycled concrete. Because the concrete is completely exposed, the concrete thermal mass stores heat and significantly reduces the requirement for active heating and cooling systems.

Left: Exterior at night with wind tower.

From left to right, from above to below:
Detail front elevation, Façade, Interior,
Interior of the wind tower.
Right: Interior of the wind tower.

VILLANUEVA PUBLIC LIBRARY,
VILLANUEVA CASANARE, COLOMBIA

CARLOS MEZA, ALEJANDRO PIÑOL,
GERMÁN RAMÍREZ, MIGUEL TORRES

www.migueltorresarquitecto.com, www.alejandropinol.com
Client: Department of Culture, **Completion:** 2007, **Gross floor area:** 2,500 m², **Photos:** Nicolas Cabrera.

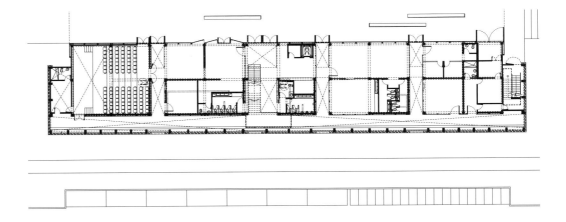

Left: Two volumes define the library. | Right: Ground floor plan.

Villanueva Public Library is the result of a national competition, won by four architecture students. The budget was tight, so low tech was the focus. The building seems just like another habitant of the landscape. It consists of two clearly defined volumes, separated visually by their material. One is clad in stone and appears to be closed, and the other one is made of wood and open. The closed volume contains the permanent space, the library, while the open space flows and functions as the urban corridor. Only local materials were used, using handcrafted and low-tech building technologies. It offers the population a place to learn, study and get a cultural education. A great example for upcoming social projects in other towns of Colombia.

From left to right, from above to below:
Wooden corridor, Wooden corridor at night, Stone wall, Interior.
Right: Stone wall during construction.

TOYO ITO & ASSOCIATES

www.toyo-ito.co.jp

Client: Tama Art University, **Completion:** 2007, **Gross floor area:** 5,639 m², **Photos:** Courtesy of the architects.

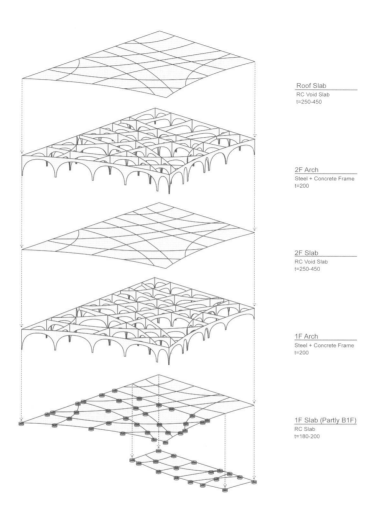

Roof Slab
RC Void Slab
t=250-450

2F Arch
Steel + Concrete Frame
t=200

2F Slab
RC Void Slab
t=250-450

1F Arch
Steel + Concrete Frame
t=200

1F Slab (Partly B1F)
RC Slab
t=180-200

Left: Exterior view at night. | Right: Axonometric.

Initially the architects proposed to place the entire library underground. After realizing that this was impossible, the volume was designed above the ground, while still trying to build a subterranean space. The building became a structural system of a series of domes and arches. The arches have been designed to follow gentle curves at different angles. These continuous curves articulate space into blocks of squares and triangles. Due to the strategic placement of the furniture, contradicting characteristics were attributed to the reading area: flow and standstill. The slope of the ground floor follows the natural declivity of the land so that the architecture is well integrated into the surrounding environment, maintaining spatial continuity between inside and outside space.

Left: View inside at night. Right: Entrance area.

HAGOP KEVORKIAN CENTER LIBRARY OF NEW YORK UNIVERSITY,
NEW YORK (NY), USA

TURETT COLLABORATIVE
ARCHITECTS

www.turettarch.com
Client: Hagop Kevorkian Center Library , **Completion:** 2003, **Gross floor area:** 119 m², **Photos:** Paul Warchol
Photography.

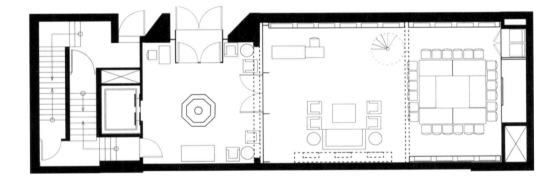

Left: View from entry hall to the stacks. | Right: Ground floor plan.

The original 1973 library incorporated architectural elements from the 1797 Quwwatli Family residence in Damascus within the noisy and drafty entry hall of a modernist Philip Johnson-designed shell. In the late 1990s, the architects separated the library acoustically and thermally from the entry with a nine meter high glass partition, with minimal impact on artisanal surfaces. Decorative elements were then restored and lighting systems were redesigned to complement historic details. The designers also created new custom desks and furnishings. The result is a bright and newly functional research and meeting space, elegantly harmonizing the historical with the modern.

255

From left to right, from above to below:
View towards entry hall, Reception desk,
View of mezzanine stacks.
Right: View towards the library.

EDIFICIO T – UPAEP,
PUEBLA, MEXICO

JOSE LUIS VARGAS WITH VARGAS
TEJEDA ARQUITECTOS,
ARQ. HUGO RAMIREZ LUNA,
ARQ. MA. EUGENIA PLATA IBARRA

www.krop.com/vtadesign
Client: Universidad Popular Autonoma del Estado de Puebla, **Completion:** 2007, **Gross floor area:** 7,200 m²,
Photos: Vargas Tejeda Arquitectos.

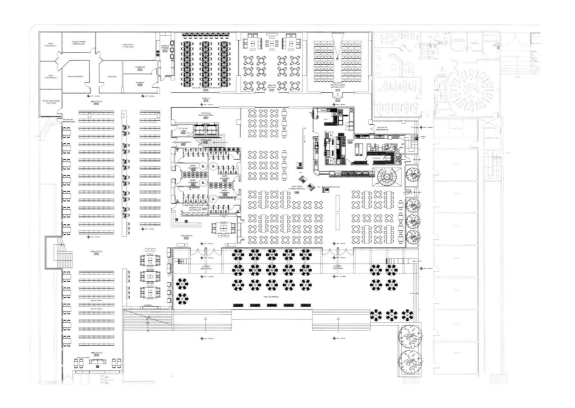

Left: Exterior perspective at night. | Right: Floor plan basement level.

The 7,200 square meter T-Library (La Biblioteca Central UPAEP) was completed in 2007, as part of a master plan to expand the university facilities, as the student population continues to grow. The new design of the T-Library opens up the interior space and brings in natural light, even to the basement level, where the new building has a connection with the pre-existing structure. The public areas facing the central campus are sheathed in glass to connote transparency and visibility – providing a visual transition of the library with its surrounding. The entrance within the ground level plaza serves as an access and distribution point, leading to a skylight-illuminated atrium which connects the other five levels of the building.

From left to right, from above to below:
Detail of the façade, Aerial view, Front view, Entrance area.
Right: Detail of entrance.

VERA OERI-LIBRARY,
MUSIC ACADEMY OF BASLE,
BASLE, SWITZERLAND

Client: Stiftung zur Förderung der Musik-Akademie der Stadt Basel, **Completion:** 2009, **Gross floor area:** 1,600 m², **Photos:** Ruedi Walti.

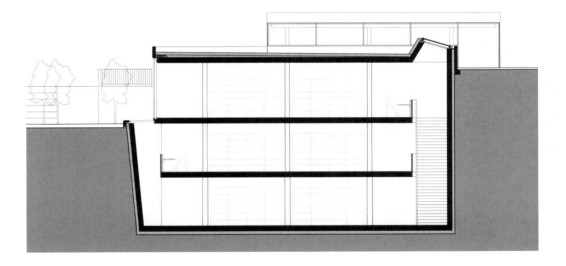

Left: View at night. | Right: Section.

The range of rooms and infrastructure in the new Music Academy library is optimally tailored to the needs of the users. The building project was realized in the form of a three story, primarily subterranean Minergie standard built structure located in the courtyard of an already existing building in the historic section of Basle. The exposure of the otherwise subterranean main building volumes on two sides of the first sublevel allows for an optimal illumination with natural light. The daylight is able to penetrate to the second and third sublevels of the library by means of two lateral overhead lighting strips. The greening of the flat roof ensures that the building nestles into the park-like surroundings.

From left to right, from above to below:
View towards the reading room at night, Reading room, Work-
staions on second basement level, Staircase with skylight.
Right: Staircase.

UNIVERSITY LIBRARY UTRECHT,
UTRECHT, THE NETHERLANDS

WIEL ARETS ARCHITECTS

www.wielaretsarchitects.nl

Client: Utrecht University, **Completion:** 2004, **Gross floor area:** 36,250 m², **Photos:** Jan Bitter.

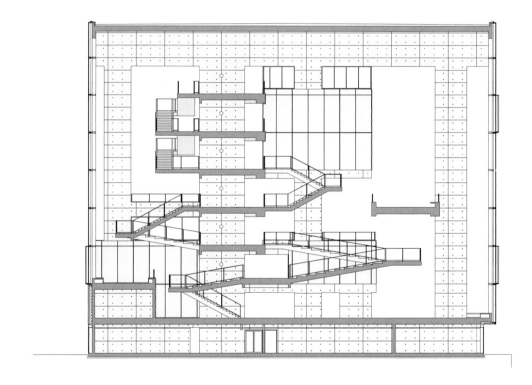

Left: Exterior view. | Right: Section.

The University Library is part of the new university complex in the city of Utrecht. The design of the library responds in an innovative manner to the paradoxical requirements of a library needing closed spaces for book storage and open spaces for public areas, like reading rooms. The closed volumes of the depots are suspended like opaque clouds in the air, yet the open structure gives visitors an experience of spaciousness. From the main entrance, a wide staircase leads to the auditorium and exhibition space and to the actual library area on the first floor. In order to reduce sunlight penetration patterns of leaves are printed onto the glazed façades and appear also inside, also creating the sense of a building in the woods.

From left to right, from above to below:
Detail of the façade, Exterior perspective, Main Staircase, View
towards the library.
Right: Workstations.

LIBRARY AND CONFERENCE CENTER, PEACE PALACE,
THE HAGUE, THE NETHERLANDS

WILFORD SCHUPP ARCHITEKTEN

www.wilfordschupp.de
Client: Carnegie-Foundation, **Completion:** 2006, **Gross floor area:** 7,600 m², **Photos:** Peter de Ruig.

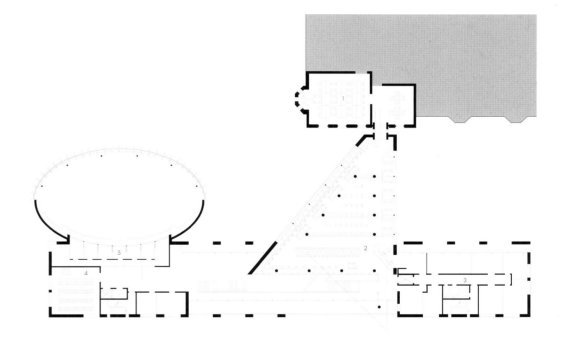

Left: View of the conference center at night. | Right: Floor plan first floor.

The building provides space for the library for international law, academy events and for court proceedings. The design exterior is marked by the connection and penetration of geometric forms: A narrow, four story cube on the south façade of the Peace Palace houses the function rooms and offices and provides access to the different areas. Its brick façade corresponds in color and materiality with the Peace Palace. The triangular library reading room „floats" as a connecting element between the new building and the palace. Another smaller reading room juts out as a wedge at the second long façade. The transverse axis of the parks points precisely to the elliptical conference hall of the new building.

Left: View of the ensemble. Right: Reading room.

From left to right, from above to below:
Reading room, View towards the foyer, Interior view of the reading
room, Detail of the façade.
Right: Conference room.

MUNICIPAL LIBRARY GRAZ ZANKLHOF,
GRAZ, AUSTRIA

IRMFRIED WINDBICHLER

www.windbichler-arch.com
Client: City of Graz, **Completion:** 2005, **Gross floor area:** 655 m², **Photos:** studio palazzo inzaghi.

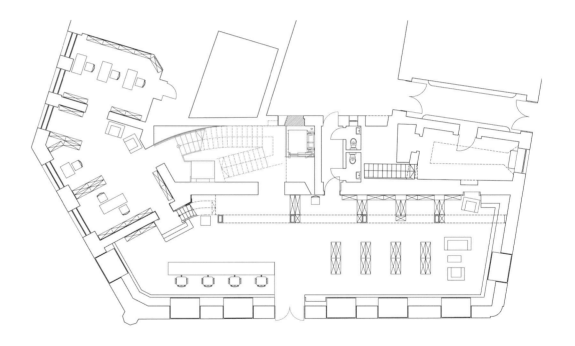

Left: View from the first floor. | Right: Layout plan ground floor.

In 1908 in the place of three smaller houses a residential and office building was built for the paint manufactuerer Zankl in the historicist style. A part of the original wooden furniture belonging to the paint outlet has been preserved on the ground floor with recessed gallery which today houses the extension of the municipal library. In 2005 a light steel stairway and an elevator were installed in the former paint warehouse, whereby the first floor was connected with the reception area and integrated in the library rooms. This represents a definitely contemporary albeit gentle intervention in the historically listed building fabric, which was achieved with a minimal budget. The library's Media Center with internet work stations nestles in the previously unused basement.

From left to right, from above to below:
Historic façade, Staircase to the gallery on ground floor,
Reception desk.
Right: Internet workstations on basement floor.

LIBRARY IN LUCKENWALDE,
LUCKENWALDE, GERMANY

PROJEKTPARTNERSCHAFT
WRONNA FELDHUSEN FLECKEN-
STEIN

www.raumbewegung.de, www.ff-architekten.de
Client: City of Luckenwalde, **Completion:** 2008, **Gross floor area:** 2,550 m², **Photos:** Andreas Meichsner Berlin.

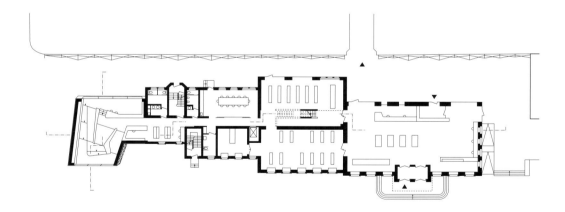

Left: Exterior view of the ensemble. | Right: Ground floor plan.

The decommissioned railroad station was renovated for the municipal library. The listed historic building received a cabinet like annex spatially tilted on two axes, locating the former train station in a new urban context. The striking façade design with the surface of shimmering gold scales underscores this urban developmental tone. The annex opens up spaces for children and youth in the interior. The renovation of the train station pursued the goal of taking into account the special atmosphere of the individual rooms with their historical materials, colors and surfaces and knitting together the patchwork fabric in a spatial continuum with a unifying color and furniture concept.

From left to right, from above to below:
Exterior view of the annex, Façade of the annex with the existing
building, Interior of the children's library.
Right: The historic train station serving as entrance area.

MULTIMEDIA LIBRARY OBERKIRCH,
OBERKIRCH, GERMANY

WURM + WURM ARCHITEKTEN UND INGENIEURE GMBH

www.wurm-wurm.de

Client: City of Oberkirch, **Completion:** 2010, **Gross floor area:** 2,100 m², **Photos:** Guido Gegg.

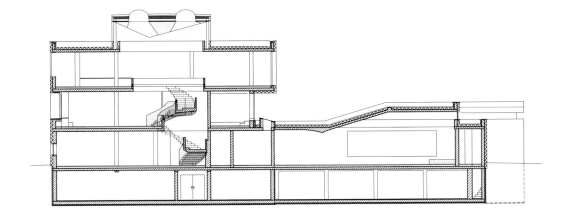

Left: South-west façade with reading garden. | Right: Section.

The multimedia library in Oberkirch is connected on three levels with an open, organically shaped stairway. Because of its central location and large skylight it also functions as a light source. The large windows serve as reading and relaxation zones, parts of which are furnished with meander shaped reading areas. In addition to the striking urban developmental architecture, special care was taken in the planning to create a high amenity value for the visitors. Throughout the building comfortable seating furniture is found which also invites the visitors to tarry in the outdoor reading terrace. The sunlight brings out the plastic modelling of the architecture from the outside.

Left: Main façade with entrance.

From left to right, from above to below:
Spiral staircase on first floor, Staircase and skylight on second
floor, Skylights seen from first floor, Detail of skylight.
Right: Reading area on first floor.

INDEX.

Imprint
The Deutsche Bibliothek lists this publication in the Deutsche Nationalbibli-
ographie; detailed bibliographical information can be found on the internet
at http://dnb.ddb.de

ISBN 978-3-03768-065-0

© 2011 by Braun Publishing AG
www.braun-publishing.ch

1st edition 2011

Selection of projects and layout: Manuela Roth
Editorial staff: Jennifer Kozak
Translation and text editing: Geoffrey Steinherz
Graphic concept: Michaela Prinz